THE SOURCE WITHIN

WHAT IF EVERYTHING YOU'RE
SEARCHING FOR IS ALREADY
WITHIN YOU?

Jeffrey Joseph Beyers

Copyright © 2025 Jeffrey Joseph Beyers
EMN8JOY Publishing
San Jose, California
All rights reserved.

No part of this book may be reproduced, stored in a retrieval system, or transmitted in any form or by any means, electronic, mechanical, photocopying, recording, or otherwise, without prior written permission of the publisher, except for the use of brief quotations in a review.

ISBN: 979-8-218-62353-1

For information, visit:

EMN8JOY.com

Table of Contents

Introduction vii

PART I: SELF – THE INNER ARCHITECT 1

Chapter 1: Awakening the Inner Creator 2

    Body Consciousness 6

    Mind Consciousness 7

    Subconscious Beliefs Shaping Reality 10

    The Power of Attention 12

    The Role of Affirmations 13

    Reclaiming Agency 14

    Transforming Your Reality 19

Chapter 2: Time, Identity, and Multidimensional Self 24

    The Dimensions of Our Reality 25

    Beyond Three Spatial Dimensions 29

    Time: A Nonlinear Dimension 31

    Multidimensional Consciousness 35

    Navigating Timelines and Free Will 38

    Reprogramming Our Perception of Time 43

    Living in Alignment with Our Higher Self 43

    The Illusion of a Fixed Identity 44

    Discovering Authenticity 45

    The Courage to Redefine Yourself 46

Chapter 3: Living in Inner Alignment 53

    Embracing the Spectrum of Experience 54

    Seeing Wholeness Instead of Separation 55

    Dissolving the Internal-External Divide 56

    Reflections and Resonance 57

    The Return to Wholeness 57

    Crossing the Threshold 58

PART II: ECHOES OF SELF AND SOURCE 63

Chapter 4: The Quantum Mirror 64

    Consciousness as the Creator of Reality 68

    Superposition and the Observer Effect 68

    The Double-Slit Experiment 70

    Unlocking Infinite Possibilities 73

    Unity and Quantum Entanglement 74

    The Energy of Identity and Attachment 75

    Aligning with the Flow of the Universe 75

Chapter 5: Reflections of Unity 81

    Archetypes and Reality 82

    Indra's Net and Infinite Reflections 84

    The Illusion of Separation 85

Chapter 6: Relationship as a Portal 90

    Seeing the Divine in Each Other 91

    The Humility of Not Knowing 91

Honoring the Source Within Others 92

Relationships as Mirrors 93

Seeing the Spark of Source in Others 93

A Unified Humanity 94

Part III: SOURCE – The Infinite Now 99

Chapter 7: Merging with the Infinite 100

The Eternal Present Moment 101

Unity Beneath Diversity 102

The Presence That Holds It All 103

Embodying Source 104

Chapter 8: The Unified Source 108

A Living Blueprint 108

The Pattern of Expression and Return 110

The Great Awakening 113

Chapter 9: Living the Sacred Pattern 119

The Fractal Nature of Consciousness 119

Personal Growth as Cosmic Evolution 123

Demonstrating Your Authenticity 124

Crossing the Threshold 130

Embracing the Infinite Possibilities 132

The Next Adventure 133

Epilogue: You Are the Source 138

Introduction

From as early as I can remember, I've felt deeply tuned into the world in ways others didn't seem to notice. Subtle things would leap out at me—smells, sensations, facial expressions, and emotions that went unrecognized by those around me. I could read people on a deeper level. I could feel things about them they hadn't said. I didn't just sense others' emotions—I felt them as if they were my own. This heightened perception might sound like a gift—and sometimes, it is—but more often, it felt like a burden. Like living in a world where everyone else was watching a black-and-white tube television, while I was dropped into an IMAX theater with surround sound shaking my seat. It was intense, and often overwhelming.

As a kid, I wasn't particularly fond of going to church on Sundays, but we went as a family regularly. I remember moments during mass when I would feel a sensation in my body that was so expansive, it made me dizzy. It was like my awareness was stretching far beyond my body. Sometimes, it became so much that I'd excuse myself and sit outside until the feeling passed.

That sensitivity became my gateway to something deeper. It stirred questions in me that couldn't be answered with surface explanations. We live in a world saturated with opinions, religious dogma, and cultural conditioning—but even as a child, I took all those answers with a grain of salt. I was curious in a way that felt constant, hungry. I wasn't willing to accept something just because I was told it was true. I needed to feel it for myself.

By the age of ten, I was already fascinated by ideas like reincarnation, life after death, and the paranormal. I had a deep sense that our true nature was spiritual, not physical—and that we existed before and after this current life.

By sixteen, the Internet wasn't what it is today, but I had something better at the time: a driver's license and access to every spiritual bookstore in the area. I devoured everything I could—books on Eastern and Western philosophy, world religions, mysticism, psychology, and quantum theory. I looked for patterns. I wanted to see what connected all the wisdom traditions, and where they overlapped.

I excelled in math and science, graduated with honors from a competitive high school, and eventually entered a PhD program in psychology, where I kept asking big questions. It became clear to me that the human experience is more than biology or environment—it's a fusion of body, mind, and spirit. Behind everything we call science or psychology is a deeper intelligence—a spiritual design that connects all things.

We are all part of something greater than ourselves. To exist alone in empty space, surrounded by nothing, would be pointless. But to live in a universe full of wonder, beauty, chaos, and synchronicity—that's where the magic happens. We are not just passive observers. We are co-creators. Our thoughts, beliefs, and intentions shape the fabric of our reality. Whether we realize it or not, we are always participating in the unfolding of life and consciousness.

That's why identity matters. Who we think we are defines how we see and show up in the world. But here's the thing: Many of the identities we hold aren't even ours. They've been handed down by family, society, and culture. We entered this world without knowing who we are, and naturally looked to others for direction. But over time, those beliefs we adopted can become limiting. They shrink our sense of possibility. We forget our vastness. We forget our truth.

Science and religion both offer frameworks to help us understand the world and our place within it. At their worst, they become rigid and dogmatic. But at their best, they offer insight and meaning. I've come to believe that true science and pure spiritual teaching are not in conflict. They are two languages describing the same truth. Strip away the ego and fear, and both paths whisper the same message: you and the universe are more powerful, more connected, and more divine than you've been led to believe.

At our core, we humans are simple in our desires. We want joy. We want connection. What if I told you that joy and connection are your natural state? That they emerge effortlessly when you're aligned with yourself and the world around you? The deeper your connection to everything—the people, the trees, the stars, your own breath—the more clearly you see: We are not separate. The divisions we experience through time, space, and identity are illusions. The truth is—we are One.

There's a longing inside many of us. A quiet pull to understand who we are and why we're here. We look to science. We look to spirituality. We look to books, teachers, podcasts, and even online shopping for those answers. I certainly did. But over time, I came to realize that the real answers live within.

I'm not claiming to have discovered the ultimate truth or the grand unified theory of life. But I have compiled what I believe are essential insights—pieces of understanding that can help us remember who we are and how this universe operates—both around us and within us. I've spent years diving into ancient texts, modern science, psychology, and personal practice. This book is a distillation of that journey.

If you've ever felt like there's more to this life than what we've been taught, this book is for you. If you're on a spiritual path and looking for clarity, think of this as your shortcut or your reminder. If you already live with a deep awareness of your sovereign self, may this be a mirror of what you already know. Either way, this book has found you for a reason. My hope is that by the end, the reason becomes clear.

This book is a road map. A guide to your spiritual nature. A framework for remembering your eternal self, and a way to navigate life in alignment, freedom, and joy. It's built on a simple SOS model: Self, Other, and Source. These three pillars guide our return to wholeness. We begin by connecting with Self—our authentic, eternal nature. Then we connect with the Other—not just other people, but everything that appears outside of us: the world, our relationships, our experiences, even our challenges. All of it is a reflection of divinity, inviting us into deeper awareness. Finally, we return to Source—the infinite consciousness that flows through it all. And in that remembering, we see the truth: Self, Other, and Source were never separate. They are One.

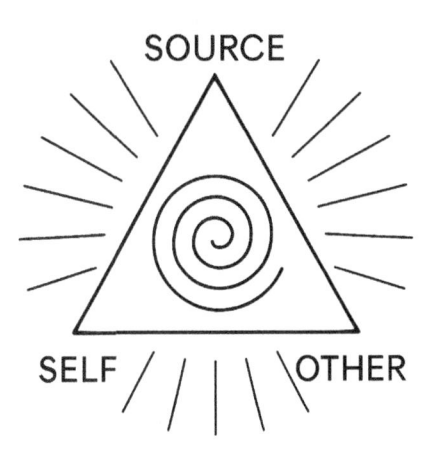

But this journey starts within. You must begin by unraveling who you think you are. Dig deep enough, and you'll remember: You are an eternal, indestructible part of Source itself. You are fully worthy of love and joy—not someday, but now.

As your beliefs about yourself shift, so will your perception of the world around you. You'll begin to see that linear time is just one perspective, and three-dimensional thinking is only part of the picture. You'll awaken to greater possibilities. And with this new perspective, your connection to others will deepen. You'll see through the illusion of separation. You'll recognize the spiral of growth that connects all beings, and all of life.

Nearly every major religion has a mystical tradition—a deeper, often hidden set of teachings that point to union rather than separation. I have studied many of them. In past ages, these teachings were often kept secret, reserved for those who were ready. They spoke not of hierarchy or sin, but of inner divinity. They told the truth that many institutions feared: God is not outside of you. God is within you. You are God, expressed in form.

Let me be clear—the term *God* we are used to hearing in most contexts is too small of a concept. Too often, it's been distorted into the image of a judgmental, external deity and used to control the masses through fear. There absolutely is something greater than us—but it is not separate. It is vast, loving, and beyond what we can fully imagine. People call it many names: God, the All, the

One, the Universe, the Great Spirit, the Infinite, Mother Nature, the Divine, Collective Consciousness, the Tao, the Field, among countless others. For the purpose of this book, I will use the term Source to describe this presence.

Source is the origin and essence of all that exists. It is the infinite intelligence, the creative force, and the unifying presence behind all life, matter, and consciousness. Source is not bound by name, image, or tradition—it is both personal and universal. It is the formless and the formed, the nameless and the known. Some feel it in nature. Others in sacred texts. Some in silence, meditation, or intuition. It is the breath behind the breath. The love beneath all form. The intelligence that creates galaxies and stirs your deepest knowing. To know Source is not to understand a concept, but to remember what you are already made of.

Throughout this book, I'll weave together teachings from spiritual traditions, science, psychology, and direct experience. My goal is to simplify what can feel complex, and offer you tools you can use—not just to understand, but to live differently.

There are exercises along the way. Take them at your own pace. Let the ideas settle in your body, not just your mind. Reflect. Question. Try them on. This isn't about adopting a new belief system—it's about reclaiming what's already yours.

I won't promise you transformation. But I will promise this: The time, energy, and attention you give to knowing yourself—and your place in this universe—is never wasted. In fact, it is the most worthwhile investment you'll ever make. You are more powerful, more eternal, and more divinely connected than you've ever been led to believe.

Part I

SELF – The Inner Architect

"You are not a drop in the ocean.
You are the entire ocean in a drop."
—Rumi

CHAPTER 1

Awakening the Inner Creator

What if your life isn't happening to you—but through you? What if the chaos, the beauty, the repetition, and the breakthrough are all echoing the same invitation: to wake up to the truth that you are not just a participant in reality, but a powerful creator of it?

I didn't always see things this way. For a long time, life felt random—sometimes magical, more often frustrating. I'd go through stretches where it seemed like the world was conspiring against me: rude strangers, unexpected roadblocks, repeating emotional patterns I swore I'd outgrown. Then one day, after yet another triggering moment that pushed me to the edge, I asked out loud, "Why does this keep happening?" The answer didn't come from outside—it rose up from within. "You're seeing what you expect to see." That single sentence cracked something open in me. It wasn't life that needed to change first. It was me.

That realization didn't make everything easier—but it made everything clearer. I began to understand that my inner world was shaping my outer reality. My thoughts were not just passing ideas—they were blueprints. My beliefs weren't background noise—they were the lens through which I experienced the world. And most surprisingly of all, many of those beliefs weren't even mine to begin with.

This wasn't about ignoring problems or pretending everything was fine. It was about reclaiming the power of perception—learning that I'm not just a passive receiver of life, but an active participant in shaping how it unfolds for me.

That's when I got really curious about the mechanics behind this. What was actually happening in the brain and mind when I shifted my attention? I dove into neuroscience, psychology, even quantum physics. What I uncovered was nothing short of mind-altering. Our brains are wired to filter reality based on what we already believe to be true. It's a set of nerve pathways called the reticular activating system—a sort of filter in our brain stem that sifts through all the data we receive and highlights what matches our internal model.

It's like your brain is constantly saying, "Oh, you think the world is stressful? Here, let me show you more proof of that." Or, on the flip side, "You believe love is everywhere? Cool, here's some evidence." This is why affirmations, belief rewiring, and conscious attention matter so much. They aren't about wishful thinking. They're about recalibrating your filter—tuning your consciousness to a different frequency. And here's the real kicker:

Most of the beliefs running our show aren't even ours. They were force-fed to us—from parents, teachers, religion, media. We internalized them before we had the capacity to evaluate or reject them. That's where the subconscious steps in, silently scripting much of our experience without our permission.

But once we bring awareness to these patterns, we gain the power to rewrite them.

For example, research in cognitive psychology demonstrates how attention and belief can dramatically shape perception. In a famous study by Daniel Simons and Christopher Chabris, participants were asked to watch a video of people passing a basketball and to count the number of passes. While doing so, most participants failed to notice a person in a gorilla suit walking through the scene. This experiment, often referred to as the "Invisible Gorilla" experiment, illustrates how attention and focus narrow our perception, causing us to overlook significant elements of our environment. In this case, the participants' belief that they were focused on counting passes led them to miss the gorilla, showing how our beliefs and focus can literally change the way we experience reality. How many times have you been deep in thought or on the phone and didn't even realize you walked past a gorilla? You'll never know.

Similarly, research in neuroplasticity shows how our subconscious programming—the automatic patterns and beliefs formed over time—can shape the way we interpret the world. Dr. Norman

Doidge, in his book *The Brain That Changes Itself,* describes how the brain can "reprogram" itself based on new experiences. For example, patients with brain injuries or sensory impairments have been shown to recover or adapt by forming new neural pathways, which illustrates how the mind can reshape itself with the right focus and intention. I saw this with my own eyes the day after my father had a stroke. He could barely read the words in a children's book and certainly couldn't understand them. He knew he was with family but he didn't remember our names. Months later he was back at running his businesses and drafting large and complex business agreements. This supports Dr. Doidge's assertion that our internal wiring and perception of reality are malleable and can be changed through conscious effort. There is always an opportunity to drastically improve our neural pathways and our inner perceptions.

When we observe any given moment, our mind processes it through layers of perception influenced by our internal beliefs and experiences. If our belief system tells us that certain things are dangerous, we will perceive potential threats more acutely. This is reflected in the work of psychologist Aaron Beck, who developed cognitive therapy, showing that people with anxiety or depression often perceive neutral or ambiguous situations as threatening. Conversely, if we hold positive beliefs about life, our perceptions will lean toward seeing opportunities rather than obstacles. The nature of consciousness, therefore, is not passive; it is actively engaged in creating the world we live in. By shifting our beliefs and becoming more mindful of our attention, we can begin to reprogram the mind, fostering a more expansive and harmonious perception of reality.

Body Consciousness

Our physical state plays a critical role in shaping our conscious experience. When we are tired, hungry, or sick, our perceptions are often clouded by discomfort. I am included in the list of people I know who think, feel, and act far from perfect when we are tired or hungry. Being "hangry" is an example of how the body influences the mind, narrowing focus to immediate physical needs at the sake of others. However, when our bodies are cared for—through rest, nutrition, and exercise—it becomes a vehicle for greater mental clarity and expanded consciousness. After a restful night's sleep or a refreshing walk in nature, the mind tends to shift to a more expansive and positive state, with clearer insights and more positive outlooks.

The interconnectedness between mind and body shows that consciousness is not just an abstract, detached experience but is deeply rooted in our physical state. Caring for the body, therefore, is an essential aspect of maintaining a vibrant, open consciousness. This idea is found in many spiritual traditions, where the health of the body is seen as a reflection of the health of the mind and spirit.

When we take a moment to slow down and tune into the inner workings of the body, we begin to notice the remarkable harmony that exists within. The breath, for example, flows in and out, steady and rhythmic, supplying life-giving oxygen to every cell. The heart pulses with a gentle consistency, circulating blood throughout the body to nourish organs and tissues. The digestive system works tirelessly to process food, turning it into energy, while the kidneys filter waste and help maintain fluid balance. All of these systems function in tandem, constantly adjusting and recalibrating to maintain equilibrium. If one system falls out of balance—such as when the heart races due to stress or digestion becomes sluggish due to poor diet—it can have a ripple effect, influencing the entire body. This delicate interconnection reveals how the body, like the universe, seeks harmony and balance, constantly working to restore order when disturbed. By paying attention to these subtle cues and tending to our physical needs, we honor the intricate design that supports our consciousness and well-being.

Mind Consciousness

Just as our physical body has a direct impact on how we feel and experience the world, so too does the mind—often in even deeper, more invisible ways. While the body broadcasts its needs loudly (hunger pangs, tired eyes, aching muscles), the mind tends to operate quietly in the background, subtly shaping our entire reality through thoughts, beliefs, and perceptions.

At first glance, thoughts seem pretty straightforward: You think them, you're aware of them, end of story. But if you've ever paid attention to your internal dialogue for even a few minutes, you know it's not always that simple. Have you ever caught yourself replaying an awkward conversation, editing your responses after the fact to deliver the perfect witty comeback? (I know I have—probably more times than I care to admit.) That mental rehashing isn't random—it's a reflection of deeper mental patterns at work.

Our thoughts don't appear out of thin air. They're generated from frameworks built over years—through upbringing, culture, education, personal experiences, and even media exposure. These internal frameworks operate like filters, coloring the way we interpret everything around us. And more often than not, we're running on autopilot, unaware of just how much these old programs dictate our present experience.

At the most basic level, our thoughts reflect how we speak. For example, my native language is English. I think in English. I remember sitting in high school Spanish class and it dawned on me that people who speak different languages *think* in those languages. I felt silly for not having thought that before, but it became so apparent to me that everyone has their own unique patterns of thought, from their language to their tone and focus.

It's worth asking: What tone does your self-talk carry? Are you quick to criticize yourself? Do you expect perfection from others—or from yourself—and beat yourself up when you fall short? The first step toward reclaiming your mind's creative power is simply noticing these patterns without judgment. Like a curious scientist observing a phenomenon, you can begin to ask:

"Is this thought truly mine, or is it something I absorbed without questioning?"

Let's take a simple example. Suppose someone cuts you off in traffic. Your mind instantly assigns meaning to that event—"That guy is rude!"—triggering a flash of anger. But where did that instant judgment come from? It's drawn from your internalized ideas about acceptable behavior. Someone else, with a different mental framework (maybe someone more relaxed or who grew up in a different environment), might shrug it off and keep singing along to their music.

I've had many opportunities to watch this dynamic at play firsthand. One of my favorite traditions is joining my wife's extended family for lively Sunday dim sum brunches. If you've ever been to a bustling Chinese restaurant, you know it's an experience: steaming carts weaving through tight aisles, plates clattering, lively conversations booming from every table—and yes, a lot of slurping sounds. At first, my Western programming flagged all that slurping as "rude." But then I learned: In Chinese culture, slurping is actually a compliment to the chef—it's a sign you're enjoying the meal. Once I shifted my perception, I wasn't bothered at all. I leaned in, smiled, and enjoyed the noisy, beautiful chaos for what it was—a celebration of life and connection.

The mind's interpretations are powerful, but they aren't set in stone. When we bring awareness to our thoughts—and stay open to reframing them—we create space for greater freedom, peace, and joy. Our consciousness becomes less reactive and more expansive.

And that's where things really start to get interesting, because just beneath the surface of our everyday thoughts lies an even deeper layer of influence: the subconscious mind. This is where the most deeply rooted beliefs live—beliefs that were often installed in us long before we had the awareness to question them.

Subconscious Beliefs Shaping Reality

Just beneath our conscious awareness resides this deeper layer—the subconscious mind. It's here that most of our core mental programming takes root, often without us even realizing it. From the time we're small, we absorb ideas about how the world works and who we're supposed to be, contributing to the layers of our internal operating system.

This conditioning isn't inherently bad. In fact, it serves important purposes: teaching us how to survive, how to interact with others, how to belong. But it can also quietly limit our sense of what's possible. The beliefs we inherit early on often go unchallenged, silently influencing the choices we make and how we perceive ourselves and the world around us.

Take, for example, society's definition of success. We're often taught—explicitly or subtly—that success looks like material wealth, social status, and physical attractiveness. Over time, these ideals can burrow deep into our subconscious, quietly steering our ambitions and measuring our worth by external markers. Media, advertising, and social narratives reinforce these messages constantly, making it easy to forget that they aren't universal truths—they're just superficial imprints that we unconsciously internalize.

I learned this lesson the hard way. A few years back, I hit a wall in my career. I was frustrated, burned out, and consumed by the nagging thought: "I should be further ahead by now. I should be making more money. I should have a bigger title." At the time, I didn't realize that the pressure I was putting on myself was rooted in old programming—expectations I had never actually chosen for myself.

The breakthrough came in two parts. First, I realized I had been pouring so much of my energy into work that I had sidelined the things that truly brought lasting joy—my health, my sanity, my relationships with family and friends. I had a long talk with myself about what really matters to me. When I shifted my focus back to those core pillars, the tight grip I had around work loosened. I started feeling lighter, more whole.

Second, I let go of the belief that my worth was tied to my career achievements. Once that pressure dissolved, something amazing happened: I relaxed. And when I relaxed, things naturally started falling into place. Ironically, when I stopped obsessing over the promotion and focused on what truly matters to me, the promotion came.

Wealth, recognition, and success aren't inherently bad. They can be beautiful, fulfilling parts of life. But they're healthiest when they flow naturally from living authentically—not from chasing standards we never consciously chose. True fulfillment comes from aligning our lives with what genuinely lights us up—not what we think is supposed to light us up.

The Power of Attention

One of the most important tools we have for shaping our reality is our attention. Attention is powerful because it's limited—we can only focus on so much at once. And what we consistently focus on becomes the lens through which we experience the world.

The tricky part? Our attention is often hijacked by our subconscious programming. If you're constantly worried about money, your brain will spotlight every bill, every expense, every story about financial struggle. If you focus on love and connection, suddenly you'll start noticing kindness in unexpected places—a warm smile from a stranger, a friend's unexpected text, a neighbor's small act of generosity.

This isn't magical thinking; it's basic brain mechanics. Our minds are wired to reinforce what we believe is important, whether it's empowering or limiting. The good news is that we're not powerless in this. We can consciously choose to redirect our attention.

It starts with awareness. What are you focusing on? Does it align with what you truly want to experience more of? If not, you have the power to shift it. Attention is like sunlight. Wherever you shine it, things grow. The question is: What are you growing?

The Role of Affirmations

One of the simplest and most powerful ways to steer your attention is through affirmations. Affirmations aren't just feel-good phrases; they are deliberate recalibrations of your internal compass.

When you affirm something like, "I am worthy of love and success," you're sending a clear signal to your subconscious mind: This is the new truth we're working with. Over time, these repeated messages build new neural pathways, gradually replacing the old limiting beliefs that once ran the show.

At first, affirmations might feel awkward or even fake. That's normal. You're introducing a new program into a system that's been running on outdated software. But just like learning a new skill, repetition and consistency are key. The more you affirm your truth, the more your thoughts, feelings, and actions begin to align with it—and eventually, your external reality does too.

It's not about pretending life is perfect. You have the power to build a deeper, more empowering narrative—one grounded in awareness and intention. Every thought you choose can be a step toward the life you were always capable of creating.

Reclaiming Agency

The real gift of this inner work is reclaiming agency. But what exactly does that mean? Agency is the recognition—and eventually, the lived experience—that you have the power to choose. It's the understanding that you're not just a passenger in life, carried along by old habits, subconscious programming, or external circumstances. You are the driver. You get to decide which direction to steer your attention, how you interpret your experiences, and what meaning you assign to events. Without agency, life feels like it's happening to us. With agency, life begins to happen through us—shaped by conscious intention and aligned with who we really are.

When you reclaim agency over your attention, you realize you don't have to focus on every fear, distraction, or drama that crosses your path. It's like flipping through radio stations—you get to choose which one you want to tune into. When you reclaim agency over your perceptions, you stop automatically assigning meaning to events based on outdated mental scripts. You start seeing things with fresh eyes, bringing curiosity and compassion instead of judgment. And when you reclaim agency over your beliefs, you step out of the heavy shadow of outdated narratives about who you're supposed to be. You begin to write your own story—one that's authentic, evolving, and true to who you are now, not who you were told to become.

This shift isn't about achieving some perfect state where nothing ever challenges you. Challenges will still come—life will still throw curveballs. But agency changes how you meet those moments. Instead of reacting automatically, you respond intentionally. Instead of feeling like a leaf tossed in the wind, you become the captain adjusting your sails. When I first realized this, it felt like a massive weight lifted off my shoulders. It wasn't that life got easier overnight—but I stopped feeling powerless, and that made all the difference.

At the center of all of this is intention. When your attention, perceptions, and beliefs are consciously aligned with your true nature, life stops feeling like a series of random events happening at you and starts feeling like something you are actively creating—with care, with clarity, and with joy. You're no longer blindly reacting to life; you're engaging with it, shaping it, evolving through it. You're remembering that you are—and always have been—a living expression of awareness, sculpting your path from the inside out.

This process is illustrated by the diagram shown here. Think of it like a pyramid: At the foundation are your beliefs. Those beliefs create your perception of reality, which filters what you pay attention to, which then shapes your perceived reality—and ultimately, defines your experience of the present moment. All of this unfolds within a broader field of awareness: conscious awareness at the surface, and the subconscious running quietly underneath.

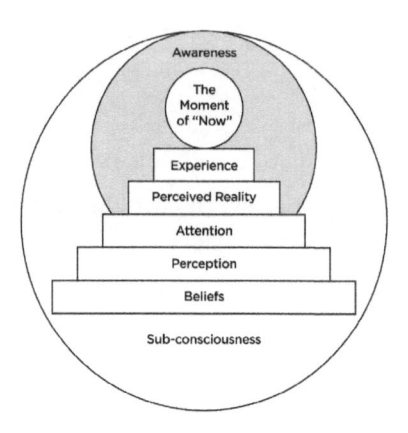

Awareness
The Moment of "Now"
Experience
Perceived Reality
Attention
Perception
Beliefs
Sub-consciousness

In the first chart, the pyramid is surrounded by two circles that represent levels of awareness. The darker, inner circle corresponds to conscious awareness. This is the space where we are aware of the present moment, our current experiences, and the perceived reality that stems from them. However, conscious awareness typically does not extend further—it stops at the surface. The larger circle represents the subconscious, which encompasses layers of influence, such as beliefs and perceptions, that shape our reality without us actively noticing them.

Most of us operate only within the surface levels—stuck in the experience of now, reacting to whatever is happening, without questioning the deeper layers influencing us. It's like only seeing the tip of the iceberg. But the truth is, there's a vast structure underneath that's shaping what we experience. When I started mapping my own patterns this way—tracing experiences back to perceptions, and perceptions back to beliefs—I saw just how much of my reality I was unconsciously creating. It was both humbling and incredibly empowering.

For example, consider your breathing. Most of the time, your breathing operates subconsciously; you are not actively aware of it. However, when you expand your awareness to focus on your breath, you can consciously alter it—slowing it down, speeding it up, or even holding it. This principle applies to the deeper layers of the pyramid as well. By expanding your conscious awareness into the subconscious layers, you can trace the connections between your experiences, perceptions, and beliefs. This self-inquiry allows you to better understand the mechanisms shaping your reality and experiences.

If you lack awareness of these deeper layers, you exist only in the surface experience of the present moment, carried along by external forces like a feather blowing in the wind. But by consciously exploring how your beliefs influence your perceptions and how those perceptions guide your attention, you can gain agency over every layer of the pyramid. This expanded awareness grants you the ability to not only understand your beliefs but also transform them, enabling greater fluidity and intentionality in your engagement with the world.

At the core of this hierarchy, awareness and agency over your beliefs is key. When you cultivate openness and a willingness to examine and expand your beliefs, you create the foundation for a more empowered and intentional relationship with the present moment. With this awareness, the "moment of now" becomes a space of possibility rather than a series of unconscious reactions.

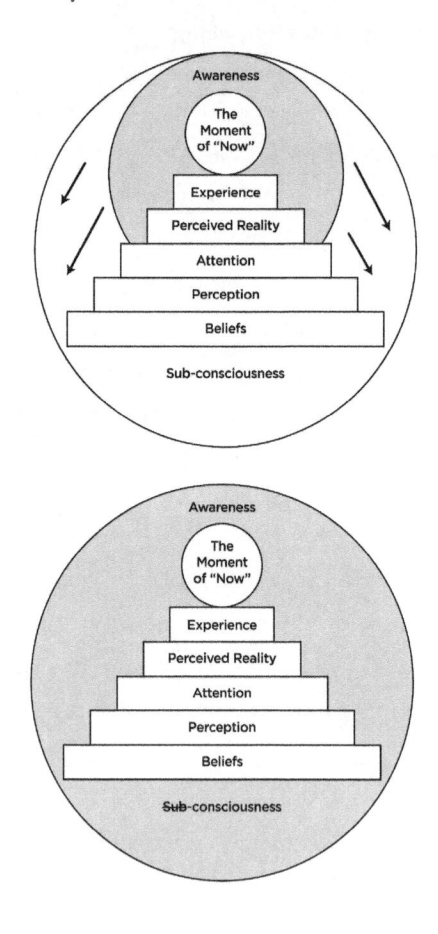

As you draw your attention to your beliefs and perceptions, your span of awareness expands. Your previously hidden beliefs and perceptions no longer reside in your subconsciousness. Your awareness of your subconsciousness then no longer makes it "sub" consciousness; it is interwoven into your conscious awareness. As your awareness expands by focusing your attention on your beliefs and perceptions, you gain mastery of your entirety, step into your power, and have full autonomy over your being.

Agency over your attention, perceptions, and beliefs leads to greater awareness and personal empowerment. Achieving this requires consistent practice and self-reflection. You must be willing to examine your beliefs and ask critical questions: What truly holds value in your life? What beliefs have you adopted over time that no longer serve you? Although these questions can be challenging, they are essential for reclaiming your power and consciously shaping your reality.

Transforming Your Reality

Understanding the relationship between consciousness, perception, and attention unlocks the potential for true transformation. With intentional focus, affirmations, and conscious self-reflection, you can begin to reprogram the frameworks that have quietly shaped your life until now.

The key realization is this: you are not a passive observer of reality—you are an active participant in creating it.

By taking ownership of your beliefs, directing your attention with care, and expanding your consciousness, you begin to build a life that aligns with your deepest desires and highest potential. This is an ongoing journey—one that calls for patience, compassion, and persistence. But every step you take toward greater clarity and intentionality brings you closer to living the life you were always meant to live.

When you harness the power of your consciousness and attention, you don't just change how you see the world—you change the world itself, starting from within.

Core Messages

1. **You are not a passive observer—you are an active creator of your reality.** Your beliefs, perceptions, and attention shape how you experience the world around you.

2. The subconscious mind quietly drives much of your experience—until you bring awareness to it. Once noticed, old programming can be rewritten with conscious intention.

3. **Where your attention goes, your reality grows.** Directing attention toward what you want to cultivate changes both your perception and your actual experience.

4. **Your physical state influences your mental and emotional state.** Caring for the body enhances clarity, consciousness, and emotional balance.

5. **Affirmations and conscious reflection help reprogram limiting beliefs.** They act as tools to expand awareness and reclaim agency over your internal world.

Affirmations

- "I am the author of my inner world and the architect of my reality."
- "I choose to focus on peace, possibility, and purpose."
- "My awareness transforms unconscious patterns into conscious power."

- "Every moment is an opportunity to redirect my attention and reclaim my truth."
- "I honor my body as a sacred partner in expanding my consciousness."

Practice: "Your Reality Filter Reset"

Objective: Rewire perception through conscious attention and daily reframing.

Time: 15 minutes a day, for 5 days.

Steps:

1. Morning Intention:

Write down *one* emotion or experience you want to cultivate more of today (e.g., peace, beauty, connection).

2. Daily Reframing Challenge:

Set a timer for 3 moments during the day. When it goes off:

- Pause.
- Observe your environment.
- Find *one* example that supports the intention you set.
- Snap a photo or write a note of it.

3. Evening Debrief:

Reflect on:

- What you noticed.

- How you felt.
- Any shifts in perception or emotion.

Why it works: This consciously engages the reticular activating system and begins rewiring your perceptual lens.

CHAPTER 2

Time, Identity, and Multidimensional Self

I've always had a strange relationship with reality—like something about the way we experience life didn't quite add up. One memory that still lingers in my mind happened in elementary school. I was sitting alone in the library, likely exiled there for cracking too many jokes in class. Bored and restless, I started playing around with that old childhood trick: rubbing my stomach while patting my head. At first, it felt impossible. But after a few tries, I got the hang of it—two distinct motions happening at once. That's when I had the thought: If I can move my body in two ways at once ... why can't I think two things at once?

I tried. Hard. I tried to recall what happened at recess while also thinking about my favorite cartoon character. But no matter how I approached it, my mind couldn't hold both thoughts simultaneously. It felt unnatural—like I should be able to do it, like somewhere deep in me, I remembered what it was like to think in parallel. In that moment, something profound stirred. Just like the time I jumped off a picnic table convinced I could fly, only to be humbled by gravity and a sprained ankle, I was baffled by this invisible limitation. Not frustrated—just deeply curious.

At ten years old, I couldn't explain it, but I knew: My spirit was capable of more than my mind could grasp. I felt it in my bones—I existed before this lifetime and would continue long after it. That moment planted a seed: that our current human experience, while rich and beautiful, is only a sliver of a much greater truth.

And that's what this chapter is about—remembering that greater truth. We are not bound by the limits of linear time or fixed identity. Beneath the surface of who you think you are is a multidimensional being—one who exists across timelines, who has possibly lived countless lives, and who can access wisdom far beyond what we've been taught is possible. If you've ever felt like you're more than just a mind and a body, you're not imagining things. You're remembering.

The Dimensions of Our Reality

To better understand our multidimensionality, let's take some time to dig into dimensions and our limited perceptions. In its simplest form, a dimension is a measurable factor. It's something that can be quantified and used to describe different states of existence. For example, gender represents a dimension with male and female at opposite ends. Age is another dimension, and so on. If we look at real-world data like voting behavior, income by gender, or age, we're analyzing trends across multiple dimensions, often two at a time.

In terms of spatial dimensions, we live in a three-dimensional world. These dimensions are height, width, and depth—creating the very fabric of the physical universe we interact with daily. Imagine a two-dimensional object, like a sheet of paper. It's flat, with only length and width. A one-dimensional object, a line, exists only in one dimension. It has length, but no width or depth. If you plot these objects mathematically, a one-dimensional object would be represented on a number line (one axis), a two-dimensional object with an x and y axis, and a three-dimensional object would require an x, y, and z axis. Spatial axes, by definition, are always perpendicular to each other.

When we try to imagine a fourth spatial dimension, we hit a conceptual wall. There's no way to directly perceive a dimension that's perpendicular to the three we know. Physically, we can't see or interact with a fourth dimension, but that doesn't mean it doesn't exist. In fact, according to modern physics, there could be more dimensions than our senses are simply equipped to perceive. The limits of our perception are tied to our conscious experience, which is confined to this three-dimensional reality. The notion that we exist in more dimensions beyond our current experience isn't far-fetched—it's just that our ability to perceive them is limited.

If we project multidimensional objects onto a two-dimensional plane, such as a sheet of paper, we see the following projections:

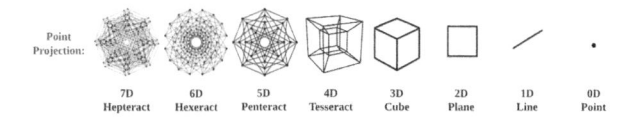

| Point Projection: | 7D Hepteract | 6D Hexeract | 5D Penteract | 4D Tesseract | 3D Cube | 2D Plane | 1D Line | 0D Point |

Our perception of the world around us is limited in profound ways, shaped by the physical constraints of our senses. The electromagnetic spectrum, for instance, extends far beyond the visible light we see, but we only perceive a very small sliver of it. Light waves, whether ultraviolet, radio, or gamma waves, are the same energy traveling at the same speed—yet their differing wavelengths lead to entirely different experiences of reality. Imagine what it would be like if we could see radio waves or microwaves. We would see them in colors we presently cannot perceive.

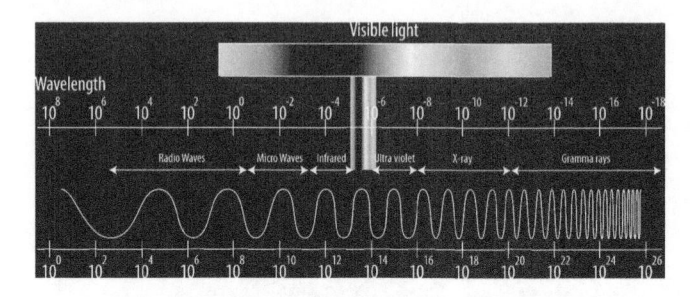

Similarly, our auditory sense is restricted to a narrow range of frequencies. While humans hear within a specific band, other creatures like elephants and whales communicate in low-frequency sounds that are inaudible to us, while insects and birds can hear higher frequencies than we can. These examples highlight how both our vision and hearing provide only limited windows into the broader, more complex spectrum of energy and information that exists around us.

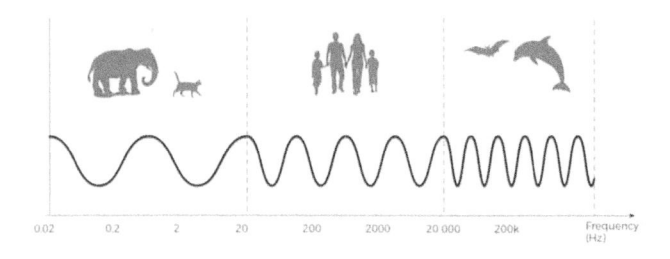

To me, it's both mind-blowing and a little humbling to realize that we're only picking up a tiny sliver of what's really happening around us. It's like we're watching reality through a basic cable package—just a few channels, decent picture, nothing too fancy—while the universe is broadcasting in full cosmic 4K with surround sound, infinite channels, and no remote to scroll through them all. There's an entire lineup of frequencies and dimensions playing in the background, and we're over here flipping between Channels 3 and 4 like, "Well, this must be everything." It makes you wonder—what else is airing on the cosmic network, just outside the reach of our current perception?

Beyond Three Spatial Dimensions

While we experience the world in three spatial dimensions—length, width, and depth—modern physics suggests there's way more going on behind the scenes. In fact, some of the most cutting-edge theories in science, like string theory and M-theory, propose that there are additional spatial dimensions folded into the fabric of reality that we simply can't perceive.

These extra dimensions aren't just some theoretical fluff either—they're believed to be mathematically necessary for the universe to function the way it does. The catch? They're "compactified," meaning they exist at unimaginably small scales, curled up so tightly that they're effectively hidden from our senses. Think of it like intricate origami tucked into the creases of space—we can't see it, but it's there, holding everything together.

Here's where it gets really fascinating. String theory says the fundamental building blocks of our universe—protons, electrons, all the stuff that makes up matter—aren't tiny dots like we once thought. Instead, they're more like vibrating strings. And the way these strings vibrate, twist, and resonate requires ten or eleven dimensions to even make mathematical sense. One model that helps us picture this is something called the Calabi-Yau manifold—basically, a mind-bending map of how those hidden dimensions might be folded in.

So why does any of this matter? Because without these extra dimensions, the math behind our most fundamental forces—like gravity and electromagnetism—falls apart. In other words, the equations scientists rely on to describe how the universe works don't fully add up unless we include more than the three dimensions we can see. That's a big deal.

Even gravity, the force that keeps your feet on the ground and planets in orbit, behaves oddly in our three-dimensional world. Compared to forces like electromagnetism, gravity is surprisingly weak. (Think about how a tiny magnet can lift a paper clip against the entire gravitational pull of the earth!) One theory, called Kaluza-Klein theory, suggests that gravity might be "leaking" into these extra dimensions—kind of like water seeping through invisible cracks in space. This could explain why it seems so much weaker here.

And that brings us to dark matter—the invisible mass that we can't see but know must be out there because of how it affects gravity and the movement of galaxies. Physicists are starting to think that dark matter might be connected to these hidden dimensions. It's like we're watching shadows dance on the wall, and even though we can't see what's casting them, we know something is there. These hidden dimensions might be influencing everything from how stars form to why galaxies spin the way they do.

This might sound like pure science fiction, but it's not—it's cutting-edge science. These models aren't just creative speculation. They're critical tools physicists use to explain why the universe behaves the way it does. The more we understand about these extra dimensions, the closer we get to answering some of the biggest questions about who we are, where we are, and how all of this is even possible.

Time: A Nonlinear Dimension

Time is often referred to as the "fourth dimension," and that is one way to make sense of the fact we can't understand or experience a true fourth spatial dimension. While we move through the world in three spatial dimensions—length, width, and height—time provides the structure that lets us track movement and change. But to really understand what this means, let's use a simple example.

Imagine a cube sitting in space. Now pick one corner of that cube—say, the back-bottom-left—and picture moving from that point to the front-top-right. You're traveling the furthest possible distance across that object. How long it takes you to make that trip depends on your speed. The math is basic: time = distance ÷ speed.

This is where time starts to reveal its true role. While we measure the world around us using spatial dimensions, time is how we measure movement through those dimensions. But here's the twist: Time itself isn't spatial. It's not something you can point to like length or depth. It's more like the rhythm behind the music of existence—it frames the tempo of life, but it's not an instrument we can touch.

And yet, time feels so real to us. It seems to flow—tick by tick—from past to present to future. But as wild as it sounds, that experience is mostly an illusion. Albert Einstein even said, "For those of us who believe in physics, the distinction between past, present, and future is only a stubbornly persistent illusion." In other words, the flow of time is something our minds create to make sense of a much more complex, interconnected reality.

The idea that time flows in one direction is deeply rooted in how we live our lives. Clocks move forward. Calendars flip pages. We age. And that gives us the feeling of linear time: a one-way journey from yesterday to today to tomorrow.

But science has a different story to tell.

Einstein's theory of relativity showed us that time is not absolute. It can stretch. It can bend. It can even slow down. Time is woven together with space into what we now call space-time—a four-dimensional fabric that doesn't behave the way we expect. The faster you move, the slower time goes. Gravity can also bend time. Get close enough to something massive—like a black hole—and time literally slows down around it.

These aren't just thought experiments. They've been tested and proven. One of the best examples is GPS. Satellites orbiting earth experience time a little differently than we do on the ground because they're moving fast and are farther from earth's gravity. If scientists didn't account for those tiny differences—using equations based on relativity—your navigation app would send you miles off course. That's how real and relevant these "mind-bending" concepts are: they're baked into the tech we use every day.

So what does this tell us? That time isn't some fixed river we're all floating down. It bends. It warps. It's not universal. And that opens the door to even stranger ideas—like the block universe theory.

In the block universe, time doesn't flow at all. Instead, every moment—past, present, and future—already exists, simultaneously. Think of it like a massive film strip. When we watch a movie, we experience a story unfolding one frame at a time. But if you unrolled the entire film strip, you'd see every scene at once. That's how the block universe views time: All moments are equally real. We just happen to be experiencing them one frame at a time.

Here's a fun analogy: Imagine watching your favorite movie. From your perspective on the couch, the story has a beginning, middle, and end. But the entire movie already exists—it's on the disk or in the stream. You just haven't watched it all yet. You're experiencing it moment by moment, but that doesn't mean the rest isn't already there. Now take that idea and apply it to your life. All the moments—your childhood, your future adventures, everything—are already part of the "cosmic film reel." Your consciousness is just watching it play out in sequence.

And just like a film editor with access to the cutting room floor, there's a part of you—your higher, multidimensional self—that can zoom out and see the bigger picture. From that broader perspective, time isn't a one-way road. It's a vast terrain where every possibility, every version of you, already exists.

In dreams, we often jump from scene to scene, flying through different locations and scenarios without worrying about time or continuity. Our dream self doesn't panic when one moment we're on a beach and the next we're in a childhood memory. That's because the "operating system" of the deeper universe doesn't care about linear time. It flows more like intuition or a story than a ticking clock.

So when you feel like time is speeding up, or when a memory suddenly hits you with crystal clarity, it might not just be nostalgia—it might be your consciousness briefly tuning into a different "frame" in the film strip of your existence.

The takeaway? Time isn't what we think it is. It's not a rigid line but a flexible, multidimensional experience. And once we start to loosen our grip on the idea of time as a straight path, we open ourselves to an entirely new way of living—one that's more connected, intuitive, and attuned to the full spectrum of who we are.

Multidimensional Consciousness

To truly expand our understanding of time, we must recognize that our consciousness exists in a multidimensional way. Our experience of time, like space, is limited by the constraints of the three-dimensional reality in which we operate. But when we begin to think of our existence and consciousness as existing beyond these boundaries, we open up new possibilities for understanding our existence.

Consider the concept of reincarnation. Most people view their lives as linear—one life follows another, with each experience building upon the last. However, from a higher-dimensional perspective, all of our past, present, and future lives exist simultaneously. This reveals that consciousness operates across multiple lifetimes and realities. It's as if, instead of reading a book from cover to cover, you can jump between chapters, experiencing them in any order. This concept directly challenges the traditional understanding of time, demonstrating that everything occurs simultaneously.

You exist well beyond the bounds of three-dimensional space and linear time, and this means your consciousness exists multidimensionally—before, during, and after this lifetime. Before entering into a specific lifetime, your consciousness—your soul—chooses certain experiences within the three-dimensional world, experiences designed to challenge you, expand you, and foster deep growth. Life, from this broader perspective, isn't just a random series of events. It's a carefully orchestrated experience, a dynamic game of expansion where challenges are selected for their potential to spark awakening and transformation. It's not unlike choosing a difficult level in a video game because you know the greater the challenge, the greater the skills you'll develop. In the same way, our soul deliberately engages in the game of humanness—with all its limitations of space, time, and forgetfulness—as a means to refine itself into an even more masterful expression of consciousness.

It may not always feel like it, especially when life presents painful or seemingly unfair circumstances. But those circumstances are not random. They were placed within your path to maximize the growth and evolution of your soul. Specific people, events, and opportunities for choice were arranged like stepping stones across a river, each one offering the chance to move into greater awareness—or, sometimes, to repeat old patterns until we're ready to move beyond them.

If the idea that you chose your life challenges at the soul level feels difficult to accept, especially in the face of deep suffering, I get it. It can be hard to swallow. Yet, I encourage you to at least consider the possibility that you are far greater and far more skilled than you have been led to believe—not just slightly bigger, but unimaginably vast. You are already a master of your multidimensional nature. So much so, that you willingly chose to incarnate into a human body, to forget your mastery, and to rediscover it from scratch—proving it not just intellectually, but through lived experience. That's not a beginner's path; that's advanced-level soul work. And when I think about those born into the toughest of circumstances—poverty, illness, broken homes—I don't see brokenness; I see brilliance. I see masters choosing the most challenging routes to demonstrate the depth of their wisdom and resilience.

Just as we are more expansive than we typically realize, so too is the universe—and so is the nature of time. Time is not a single, rigid track carrying everyone forward in the same direction. Instead, there are infinite paths or timelines branching out at every moment. Each one represents a distinct succession of events, shaped by choices, thoughts, and energy. And while it may seem like we're all riding the same track together, the truth is, each of us is walking our own unique timeline—and the only one that truly matters is the one you are consciously choosing right now.

Navigating Timelines and Free Will

At each moment, we stand at a crossroads of countless possible futures that exist within the field of probabilities. Every decision we make—whether to go to work, take a hike, or even pause for reflection—sets us on a distinct path. These choices, though seemingly small, create ripples that shape our experiences and outcomes, charting the course of our lives. While we often feel as though we are simply reacting to external events, we are, in truth, the architects of the timelines we traverse. Each choice, conscious or unconscious, serves as a brushstroke on the canvas of our reality.

The concept of timelines suggests that parallel realities exist simultaneously, branching off based on the decisions we make. Quantum physics offers intriguing evidence of this through theories like the "many-worlds interpretation," which posits that every decision spawns a new branch of reality. In this framework, there are infinite versions of "you," each experiencing a different sequence of events based on the paths you've chosen—or not chosen. For example, in one reality, you might have pursued a career in medicine, while in another, you explored an entirely different vocation. These alternate versions of yourself exist not as hypothetical possibilities but as actualized outcomes in parallel dimensions. This perspective challenges the notion of a singular, linear life and invites us to consider the profound implications of every choice we make.

Now, I get it—you might be thinking, "Seriously? Infinite versions of me? Parallel realities just waiting to spin off depending on whether I order a salad or a burger at lunch?" Trust me, when I first encountered these ideas, I thought the same thing. It felt like something straight out of Marvel's multiverse movies, *Rick and Morty* episodes, or some late-night sci-fi binge where everything eventually spirals into mind-bending chaos. I mean, in everyday life, we only see one track—one story unfolding—and it's natural to think that's the only one that exists. But the more I sat with these concepts, the more I realized: Just because we don't perceive the branching paths doesn't mean they aren't real. Like invisible radio signals crisscrossing the air around us, these possibilities exist whether or not we tune into them.

If we imagine our lives as a recorded film, it would seem to follow a single, concrete narrative—a sequence of events tracing our journey from birth to the present moment. However, this apparent linearity obscures the truth: At every step, we have faced countless decisions that subtly or dramatically altered our trajectory. Each choice—whether to speak up or remain silent, to turn left or turn right—propels us into a new timeline with its own unique set of experiences and opportunities. These decisions may feel insignificant in the moment, yet they are the building blocks of our reality, forming a branching network of possibilities. As we navigate these timelines, we are not passive observers but active participants, wielding the power of free will to steer the course of our lives.

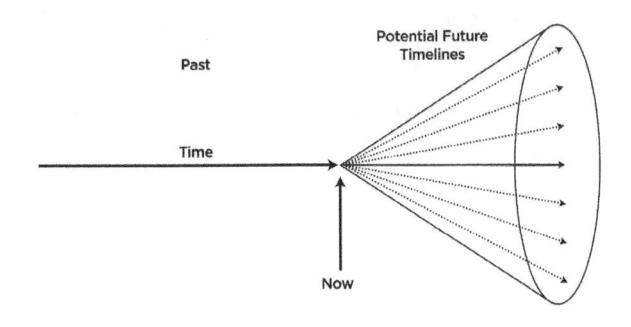

What's more, the ability to navigate timelines is not limited to the present moment. Every memory we revisit, every emotion we dwell upon, and every dream we envision has the potential to influence the timeline we are currently living. For instance, focusing on gratitude and self-compassion can redirect us toward a more positive reality, while clinging to fear or regret might draw us into less desirable outcomes. This highlights the malleability of existence: By aligning our thoughts, emotions, and actions with the future we desire, we can consciously create a timeline that resonates with our highest potential. In this sense, time is less a rigid framework and more a dynamic medium, shaped by the interplay of choice, intention, and awareness.

While we may have free will in the sense that we can make choices, we are also influenced by forces beyond our control. External factors—like natural disasters, accidents, or even societal expectations—can guide us toward certain paths. These forces often feel like they are out of our hands; yet they, too, are part of the multidimensional nature of existence. We are not simply passive participants in our lives, but active architects of the timelines we navigate.

Our human body serves as an avatar, a tangible manifestation of our soul's true essence. However, this avatar comes with inherent limitations. The physical hardware of our bodies and minds is designed to perceive the world in three-dimensional space and linear time, reinforcing a cause-and-effect mindset. Additionally, our thought processes are often dualistic, categorizing everything into binaries like "good or bad" or "right or wrong." This perspective keeps us grounded in the immediate and familiar but also narrows our ability to perceive the larger, multidimensional reality. As we explore these ideas, it's essential to recognize how deeply this programming influences our day-to-day lives and choices. By stepping beyond this mindset, we can begin to understand that the "you" we typically identify with—the body and mind—is just one aspect of a much broader and timeless essence.

The truth of our existence lies in our soul, the multidimensional self that exists beyond the constraints of space and time. If we think of the human body as a character in a video game, then the soul is the player controlling that character. Just as a gamer selects the difficulty level, objectives, and parameters of a game before playing, our soul meticulously plans the framework of each lifetime. This includes setting certain challenges, choosing key people to enter our lives, and orchestrating pivotal events that offer opportunities for growth and learning. From the perspective of the avatar, these experiences often feel random, and their purpose is obscured. But from the perspective of the soul, every challenge and joy serves a higher purpose: the expansion and evolution of our essence. This holistic view reframes life's struggles as opportunities for profound spiritual growth.

The most challenging aspect of this process is the deliberate erasure of memory that occurs when we enter a lifetime. As multidimensional beings, we "up the stakes" by choosing to forget the game's parameters, making our experiences raw, authentic, and unpredictable. This amnesia allows us to fully immerse ourselves in the journey, confronting challenges without preconceived solutions or expectations. Imagine the diminished satisfaction of solving a puzzle you already know the answer to or watching a movie where you know every outcome in advance. The beauty of life's design lies in the discovery, the uncertainty, and the growth that emerges from making choices in the face of the unknown. This deliberate forgetting ensures that our responses to life's difficulties are genuine and meaningful, allowing us to extract the maximum value from every experience. Through this lens, even life's most painful moments serve as catalysts for the soul's ultimate expansion and fulfillment.

Reprogramming Our Perception of Time

When we understand that we are multidimensional beings with the ability to navigate different timelines, we begin to see the significance of our choices. The values and beliefs we hold deeply affect the paths we take. The desires we have—whether to gain wealth, power, or prestige—are often shaped by societal expectations rather than our true soul's needs.

The deeper fulfillment we seek comes not from external achievements, but from the experiences that challenge and stretch us. True growth occurs when we embrace challenges and opportunities for learning. This process of aligning with our highest potential involves shifting away from materialistic desires and focusing on the deeper, more spiritual aspects of our being. Through this shift, we can navigate our timelines more consciously, choosing paths that resonate with our soul's true purpose.

Living in Alignment with Our Higher Self

In the end, understanding time, space, and consciousness as multidimensional concepts empowers us to live more intentionally. By recognizing that all timelines exist at once and that we are capable of shifting into those timelines, we can make conscious choices that align with our highest truth. Each moment becomes an opportunity for growth and transformation, and as we act with awareness, we navigate our journey with clarity and purpose.

The Illusion of a Fixed Identity

Our identities are often built on past experiences and beliefs—many of which limit our potential. Consider the person who says, "I'm not good at math" or "I can't ride a bike." These statements may have been true at some point, but are they eternal truths? Perhaps their struggles with math stemmed from poor teaching methods, or their inability to ride a bike was due to fear or lack of practice. These limitations, once accepted, can become self-fulfilling prophecies, reinforcing the belief that we are confined to what we have always been.

Human history tells a different story. Our ancestors ran for miles in pursuit of prey, crafted tools from raw materials, and overcame extraordinary challenges to survive and thrive. The human body and spirit are far more capable than the limitations of identity suggest. Yet, we often blind ourselves to this truth by clinging to narrow definitions of who we think we are.

Ask yourself: *Who am I?* What attributes do you cling to? How often do you begin thoughts with "I'm just a …," "I'm not …," or "I can't …"? These beliefs about your identity shape your perspective, which in turn shapes your reality. For instance, someone who identifies as a failure in relationships may unconsciously arrange their life to confirm that belief. Consciously or unconsciously, they are cutting off timelines that prove otherwise. They might avoid intimacy, sabotage connections, or misinterpret others' actions in ways that reinforce their negative self-image.

But what if, instead of saying, "I'm just a …," you declared, "I am far greater than that"? By expanding your view of who you are and letting go of outdated beliefs, you begin to loosen the illusion of a fixed identity. This opens the door to something more honest and enduring: your authentic self. Not a title, a role, or a reaction to others, but the steady inner presence that exists beneath all of that—your clearest values, your natural strengths, and your quiet knowing of what truly matters.

Discovering Authenticity

Your authentic self is the part of you that remains when all external expectations fall away. It is the version of you that feels aligned, unforced, and whole—a combination of what you care about most, what energizes you, and what feels deeply true. Like a compass, it points you toward a life of greater ease, meaning, and fulfillment. While your constructed identity may shift with time and circumstance, your authenticity is consistent, even if it takes time to uncover. Just as no two people live the same life, no two expressions of authenticity are exactly alike. Finding this authenticity is a lifelong journey, but it is the most rewarding endeavor you can undertake. When you align with your true nature, the universe responds. Life begins to flow with ease, synchronicities arise, and the path forward becomes clearer.

A powerful way to recognize whether you are living authentically is to ask: *Does this bring me joy?* Joy is a reliable indicator that you are aligned with your truest nature and optimal path. Consider the story of a person who pours their energy into curating the perfect online persona—chasing likes, followers, and the next viral moment. At first, the praise and attention feel validating, even addictive. But over time, the constant performance takes a toll. They begin to feel disconnected from who they really are, trapped in a cycle of comparison and approval-seeking. The more they strive to be what others admire, the more they lose sight of their true self. Instead of joy, they experience anxiety, exhaustion, and an inner void no amount of digital applause can fill. In seeking validation from the outside world, they overlooked the one voice that truly mattered—their own.

For the fortunate, this realization sparks a journey of self-awareness. They begin to question: *What truly brings me fulfillment? What resonates with my soul?* For others, however, the fear of confronting their misplaced priorities may lead them to cling even more tightly to their old ways. This is the paradox of self-awareness: it offers freedom, but only to those brave enough to confront their own illusions.

You are not bound by who you've been. You can choose, in this very moment, to embody a version of yourself that aligns more fully with joy, purpose, and inner truth. No permission required—only your willingness.

The Courage to Redefine Yourself

Self-awareness demands bravery. It requires loosening the grip on what you think you know about yourself and being open to the possibility that you've been off your true path. This process can be uncomfortable—it challenges the foundations of your identity and forces you to question deeply held beliefs. But on the other side of this discomfort lies the freedom to create a life that is authentically yours.

Once you begin to question what truly brings you joy, action becomes the next step. Living authentically means making conscious decisions that align with your core values and purpose. When you act from this place of alignment, the universe responds in kind. Seemingly coincidental opportunities arise, and the resources you need manifest at the perfect time. This feedback loop reinforces your journey, guiding you toward greater fulfillment and abundance.

Consider the artist who abandoned their passion for painting to pursue a more "practical" career. For years, they felt a vague sense of dissatisfaction, despite their professional success. One day, they decided to pick up a brush again—not to achieve anything grand, but simply because painting brought them joy. Over time, this small act of authenticity transformed their life. They began dedicating more time to their art, which eventually led to opportunities they never imagined—gallery exhibitions, a supportive community of fellow artists, and a renewed sense of purpose.

Recognizing and shifting into authenticity does not have to be drastic. It is incremental, a succession of countless decisions to say yes to your true nature over and over. By repeatedly recognizing and acting upon our core nature, our true essence, we are continuously shifting toward our optimal timelines. For example, if we are veering out of our lane on the highway, we don't drastically swerve our car into the middle of the lane. Instead, we slowly correct and adjust over a period of time. Building muscle or learning a new skill is no different; both take daily and continuous awareness and effort.

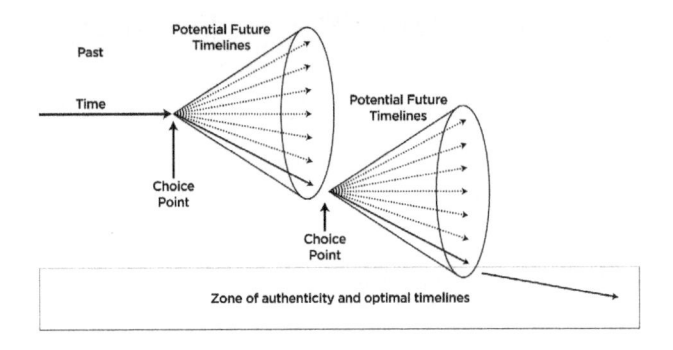

Our optimal timeline is the space within the field of probabilities in which our most pure form of consciousness and awareness resonates most. Operating within a space of full awareness and presence allows us to flow with the situations and surroundings. It manifests the greatest good for you and all. Your optimal timeline is living the life that you always imagined. You have imagined it because it lives within the realm of possible futures. However, living and being within your own core resonance, the resonance of the universe and Source, can bring futures even greater than you can imagine. Is there a time where you were driving for or hoping for a particular outcome in your life, and the universe had different plans and threw your script aside? In most likelihood, something even better resulted despite the unexpected turn of events. Consider the man who misses the last train to work only to meet his future wife at the train station.

Understanding that you are a multidimensional being—here by choice, not chance—changes everything. You are not here to survive your life. You are here to shape it. To choose timelines like doors. To walk with intention through the ones that match the truth of who you are. The version of you that lives in joy, freedom, and inner harmony isn't a fantasy—it's a frequency. It already exists. The question is: Are you tuned to it?

Because knowing who you are is one thing. Living from that knowing? That's the real work. That's where we go next.

Core Messages

1. **You are a multidimensional being, existing beyond space, time, and identity.** Your essence is not limited to this physical life—your consciousness spans timelines, lifetimes, and realities.

2. **Time is not linear; it is a flexible, multidimensional medium shaped by attention and choice.** Past, present, and future exist simultaneously like scenes in a film strip—your awareness determines what you experience.

3. **Every choice you make shifts your timeline.** Timelines aren't fixed; they branch infinitely based on your decisions, emotions, and intentions.

4. **Your identity is fluid and expansive—not fixed by past experiences.** You can redefine yourself at any moment by choosing thoughts, actions, and beliefs aligned with your authentic self.

5. **Living authentically is how you access your highest timeline.** Joy, resonance, and inner alignment are indicators that you're embodying your true multidimensional nature.

Affirmations

1. "I am a multidimensional being, free to choose my reality in every moment."

2. "Time does not confine me—I align with the timeline that honors my highest self."
3. "I am not my past; I am the creator of my present and future."
4. "I trust my inner resonance to guide me toward alignment, joy, and purpose."
5. "Every conscious choice I make opens a new path of possibility and growth."

Practice: "Parallel You Day"

Objective: Explore multidimensional identity by embodying your highest timeline.

Time: 1 day of active role-play.

Steps:

1. Identify Your Parallel Self:

Imagine a version of you who lives with purpose, peace, and alignment. Describe them in detail:

- What is their first thought when they wake up?
- How do they speak to others?
- What do they say yes or no to?
- How do they respond to challenging people or situations?

2. Embody the Role:

For one day, *become* this version of you. Make choices as they would. Speak as they would. Walk with their posture. Respond to stress from their state of mind.

3. Document the Results:

At night, reflect:

- What changed in how others responded to you?
- What parts of that identity felt most natural or empowering?

Why it works: Stepping into your core resonance creates energetic alignment with new timelines.

CHAPTER 3

Living in Inner Alignment

The journey inward doesn't end when you realize you're more than your body, your thoughts, or your past. That realization is only the doorway. What follows is the integration—learning to live from that deeper truth, to let it shape how you move, choose, and relate to the world around you. This is where the real transformation begins.

This first section of the book—the *S* in the SOS model—has been about Self. Not the constructed identity shaped by culture, family, or fear, but the deeper, eternal Self. In chapter 1, we explored how beliefs and attention shape our reality. In chapter 2, we expanded into the idea of time, identity, and the multidimensional nature of who we really are. Now, in chapter 3, we ask: How do we embody that? How do we *live* in a way that reflects that vastness, that truth?

Living in alignment doesn't mean you'll never feel doubt or face challenges. It means living in coherence—where your inner truth matches your outer expression. It's a return to your natural rhythm, where decisions flow from clarity, actions arise from intention, and life feels less like resistance and more like resonance. Alignment is not a destination; it's a practice. A choice you make moment by moment, to come back to yourself. And the more you return to yourself, the more familiar that feeling becomes. Inner alignment is not a fixed state—it's a dynamic rhythm, a conversation between your inner wisdom and the unfolding of life.

Embracing the Spectrum of Experience

We tend to see life in absolutes: good or bad, right or wrong, success or failure. But reality is far more nuanced. Between the poles lies a full spectrum—a rich, complex range of emotions, experiences, and truths. Joy and sorrow often exist side by side. Ease and effort, gratitude and frustration, calm and chaos—they all coexist within a single day, sometimes a single moment.

You might start your day with peace and end it in tension. You might love your family deeply and still feel overwhelmed by them. These aren't contradictions—they're just part of being human. Life isn't asking us to choose one feeling over another, but to make space for all of it.

This also extends to who we are. You can be deeply connected to your spiritual path and still experience fear or anxiety. You can be a compassionate person and still feel anger. Growth doesn't mean erasing these tensions—it means allowing them, witnessing them, and holding them with kindness.

Inner alignment isn't about perfection or predictability. It's about presence. It's about welcoming all aspects of yourself and your experience, knowing they belong. The sacred isn't only found in stillness and light—it's in the full, messy, vibrant spectrum of what it means to be alive.

Seeing Wholeness Instead of Separation

When you begin to live in alignment, you stop slicing the world into parts. Instead of labeling people as friend or threat, you start seeing the shared humanity underneath. The angry driver, the difficult coworker, the political opponent—they become mirrors, not monsters.

Everything you encounter becomes part of the whole, and your perception begins to soften. Compassion arises more easily. Judgments fade. You begin to feel the interconnectedness that spiritual traditions have always spoken of. Not as an idea—as a lived experience.

When you stop identifying everything and everyone as separate or "other," you begin to see the hidden web of unity underneath all things. This doesn't mean you abandon discernment, boundaries, or individuality. It means you see those distinctions within the context of wholeness, not fragmentation. You understand that while we are unique expressions of consciousness, we are made of the same essence.

The shift is subtle but radical: from division to inclusion, from alienation to empathy. You begin to listen more deeply. To feel the energy underneath the words. To see the child behind the anger, the pain behind the judgment, the soul behind the mask.

Dissolving the Internal-External Divide

We tend to think of our inner world and the outer world as separate. But they're not. The world you see is a reflection of the world you carry within. When you shift your beliefs, your energy, your attention—you shift what you experience.

Have you ever been in a great mood and noticed how people smiled more, doors opened more easily, synchronicities showed up? That wasn't luck. That was resonance. Your internal frequency was attuned to openness, and the world mirrored it back.

Conversely, when you're in a state of contraction—tense, guarded, stressed—everything seems more difficult. People appear colder. Opportunities feel scarce. The difference isn't the world. It's you. This is not about blame—it's about empowerment. Because when you change what's happening within, you reclaim the ability to influence what unfolds around you.

This insight is a bridge to mastery. It shifts you from being at the mercy of circumstances to being the artist of your experience. You realize that life isn't just happening to you—it's responding to you. That awareness is where true alignment begins.

Reflections and Resonance

We often believe we are separate from the world we observe—inside is "me," outside is "everything else." But the line between internal and external is far more fluid. The reality you experience is not objective; it's reflective. It bends to the lens you're looking through.

Your frequency shapes your encounters. Your beliefs tint your perceptions. This doesn't mean you control everything—it means you participate in everything. You're not simply reacting to life; you are in continuous, co-creative dialogue with it.

The moment you shift your inner stance—soften a judgment, release an old belief, expand your compassion—you begin to experience life differently. And this is where alignment becomes alchemy. Your internal coherence reorganizes your outer world. Peace is no longer something you chase; it's something you carry. Reality becomes a mirror, yes—but also a canvas. You are not just the reflection. You are the artist.

The Return to Wholeness

Chapters 1 through 3 have been a spiral inward—a deep reckoning with who you are beneath conditioning, time, and form. You've explored how beliefs shape your perception, how timelines shift through awareness, and how your body, mind, and soul are intimately connected across dimensions.

But this isn't just information. It's initiation.

The journey of Self is not about reaching a perfect version of you. It's about remembering what has always been true: that you are whole, now. That joy is your compass. That alignment is a practice, not a performance.

And joy isn't just a passing emotion—it's a signal. A resonance. When you feel it—not as fleeting pleasure, but as deep, subtle aliveness—it's a sign you're in contact with your essence. Joy arises not when life is perfect, but when you are present. It's the quiet "yes" that tells you: this is the way.

You were never meant to fix yourself—only to reclaim yourself. The "you" that is not defined by trauma, titles, or timelines, but by presence. The "you" that is steady beneath all seasons. That is the Self this section has pointed you back toward: not something to become, but something to live from.

Crossing the Threshold

Something happens when we begin to live in alignment. The boundary between self and surroundings softens. We no longer experience the world as something "out there" to manage or fix—but as something to meet, to listen to, to respond to with presence.

The more you know your own essence, the more clearly you perceive what exists beyond it. What once felt separate becomes part of a larger conversation. Environments speak. Symbols echo. Encounters ripple. The textures of life—relationships, patterns, synchronicities, even challenges—reveal themselves not as obstacles, but as invitations.

This is where we go next.

As you step into the next part of the journey, you won't be leaving the Self behind—you'll be expanding from it. This inner alignment becomes the foundation for how you engage with everything beyond it: not just other people, but experiences, environments, energies, and the unseen architecture of the world around you.

There is more waiting to meet you. Not because you've finished the journey inward—but because you're ready to carry it outward.

Core Messages

1. **Inner alignment is not about perfection—it is about presence.** It's the ongoing practice of returning to your center and allowing your life to flow from that grounded truth.

2. **The boundaries between inner and outer are more fluid than they appear.** Life is not happening to you—it's responding to you, echoing the energy you carry within.

3. **Your experience of reality is shaped by participation, not passivity.** When you shift internally—through awareness, compassion, or clarity—you shift how the world meets you.

4. **Joy is your inner compass.** It's not a reward for getting life right—it's a resonance that arises when you're aligned with your essence.

5. **Living from the Self is not the end of the journey—it is the beginning of how you meet the rest of existence.** From this wholeness, you engage with life more clearly, more gently, and more powerfully.

Affirmations

- I return to myself with every breath—I live from presence, not performance.

- My alignment shapes my experience; my inner coherence becomes outer clarity.
- Joy is my compass. I follow what feels alive, true, and quietly powerful.
- I trust that how I meet the world transforms what the world becomes for me.
- I am not separate from life—I am in conversation with it. I listen, I shape, I respond.

Practice: The Resonance Journal

Objective: Build self-awareness and alignment by tracking resonance through daily experience.

Time: 5–10 minutes a day, for 7 days

Steps:

1. Morning Intention:

- Set an intention: "Today, I will notice what feels aligned and what does not."

2. Throughout the Day:

- Pause after key interactions or decisions.
- Ask: *"Did that feel expansive or contractive? Aligned or off?"*
- Take mental or physical notes.

3. Evening Reflection:

- Write down 2–3 moments where you felt most alive, at ease, or joyful.
- Write down 1–2 moments where you felt drained, off, or disconnected.
- What were the common threads?

4. Weekly Insight:

- At the end of the week, look for patterns.
- What environments, people, or activities brought alignment?
- What consistently took you out of that state?
- How can you adjust your choices to reflect what brings resonance?

Why it works: Awareness precedes change. This practice trains you to tune into your inner compass and make more aligned choices from the inside out.

Part II

Echoes of Self and Source

"We are not human beings having a spiritual experience. We are spiritual beings having a human experience."
—Pierre Teilhard de Chardin

CHAPTER 4

The Quantum Mirror

In the journey of remembering who we are, the first step is inward—toward the Self. We begin there because it is the closest and most accessible part of the experience of consciousness. But the Self does not exist in a vacuum. Once we begin to awaken to our true nature, we inevitably come face-to-face with everything that seems to be not us.

This next phase of the journey—what I call the *O* in the SOS model—is about engaging with the Other.

Now, when we hear the word "other," we often think of people—strangers, friends, lovers, or enemies. And yes, other people are an essential part of this layer. But "the Other" is far more expansive than that. It includes everything in your external field: the challenges you face, the objects you interact with, the environments you live in, and the systems you're embedded within. It's the world outside the Self, the material realm as you perceive it. It's your job, your family, your body, your bank account. It's the weather and the traffic and the email that upsets you. It is everything that appears separate from you but is actually a reflection of you.

If the Self is the subject, the Other is the object—but only from the illusion of separation. As we'll explore in the next three chapters, what appears as "out there" is intricately woven into the tapestry of your inner world. The Self and the Other are not opposing forces. They are dancing partners. They inform, reflect, and refine one another. And in truth, the Other is not "other" at all. It is the Self in mirrored form—made visible, tangible, and interactive through experience.

This is a vital distinction. Because unless we understand this, we will continue to treat the world as something that happens to us rather than something that responds through us. We will keep fighting shadows, blaming circumstances, and missing the deeper truth: that everything in the Other is offering us a portal—a chance to become more conscious, more integrated, and more whole.

The chapters that follow—chapters 4, 5, and 6—are dedicated to the exploration of the Other. Not just as a philosophical idea, but as a living, breathing aspect of your reality. We will look at how the world reflects the Self back to you (chapter 4), how others reflect your internal landscape and archetypal energies (chapter 5), and how honoring the divinity in others leads to true empathy, unity, and cooperation (chapter 6).

This is where inner work becomes relational. Where insight becomes interaction. Where the rubber meets the road.

There are certain moments in life—quiet, sudden, humbling—where the world seems to shimmer with deeper meaning. Something as ordinary as sunlight through trees, a strange coincidence, or a look in a stranger's eyes begins to feel alive, as if reality itself is speaking back. It's subtle. Often fleeting. But in those moments, we sense it: The outer world is not so outer after all. Something within us is being reflected back by the world around us.

There are certain moments in life when the way you view everything—yourself, the world, reality itself—suddenly shifts. For me, learning about quantum theory was one of those moments. I had always sensed there was more to existence than what I could see or touch, but quantum physics gave me language for what I had only intuitively felt: Reality is not as solid, not as fixed, as we were taught to believe. It is shimmering, alive, full of possibility, and deeply responsive to our consciousness.

Albert Einstein's famous equation, $E=mc^2$, taught us that matter is a form of energy. And the deeper scientists have explored the atom, the more they've found that what we think of as "solid" is mostly empty space, punctuated by tiny particles of energy flickering in and out of existence. Quantum physics shows us that the universe is not made of hard, fixed objects, but of an infinite field of probabilities. Reality, at its most fundamental level, is a dance of energy, shaped by the act of observation.

At first, this concept felt completely mind-bending. But the more I sat with it, the more it resonated—not just intellectually, but viscerally. I realized I had already glimpsed this hidden nature of reality in the quiet moments of life, when intuition spoke louder than logic. Now, science was confirming it: Our consciousness isn't a passive witness to a fixed world. It's an active participant, shaping the unfolding of existence itself.

To make this idea easier to grasp, let's go back to the video game analogy, or a virtual reality world. The entire world of the game—the mountains, oceans, secret caves—doesn't fully exist on the screen until the player moves toward it. As you explore, the game's code "builds" the environment around you. The parts you aren't looking at remain in a latent, potential state, waiting for your attention to bring them to life. Our universe, according to quantum theory, operates in a similar way. It is a field of infinite possibilities, and our focus, attention, and observations collapse those potentials into tangible experiences.

This reminds me of the old philosophical question: "If a tree falls in the forest and no one is around to hear it, does it make a sound?" From a quantum perspective, the answer isn't simple. Without an observer, the event exists as a probability, not a certainty. Reality doesn't crystallize into form until it's observed.

Consciousness and observation, it turns out, are not just passive acts—they are acts of creation.

Consciousness as the Creator of Reality

If this idea seems too fantastical, think about it another way: every moment you live is a co-creation between your awareness and the infinite field of potential outcomes surrounding you.

Let's say you often hike a trail through the woods. One Saturday, the trail is clear. A week later, you return and discover a tree has fallen across the path. From one perspective, the tree must have fallen sometime during the week. But from another, more quantum perspective, the fallen tree existed in a field of potentialities—and your conscious observation in that moment collapsed it into reality.

Learning this shifted how I approached every aspect of my life. I realized I wasn't a passive character moving through a fixed world; I was an explorer in an unfinished landscape, shaping my journey step by step by where I directed my attention, energy, and belief. Every time we turn a corner—literally or figuratively—we spin the wheel of probabilities. And as we'll explore in the next chapters, we can even learn to influence that wheel toward outcomes that serve our highest good.

Superposition and the Observer Effect

Quantum mechanics reveals even more strangeness—and wonder—through the concept of superposition. In the quantum realm, particles can exist in multiple states at once. Only when they are observed do they "collapse" into a single reality.

I remember the first time I read about Schrödinger's cat. I sat there, blinking, trying to wrap my head around it. In this famous thought experiment, a cat in a sealed box is both alive and dead at the same time—until someone opens the box and observes it. Until that moment of observation, both outcomes exist simultaneously in a cloud of probability.

It sounds ridiculous, right? But as wild as it seems, the behavior of actual quantum particles mirrors this paradox. When electrons orbit a nucleus, they don't travel in neat, predictable paths like little planets. They exist in orbitals—clouds of probability—without defined locations. Only when observed do they "choose" a position.

An even simpler analogy is a spinning coin. When the coin is midair, it's not heads or tails—it's both, in a way. It's only when it lands (and we observe it) that the outcome is finalized.

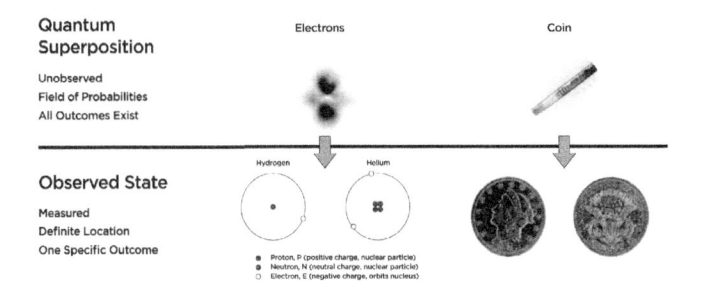

Quantum Superposition	Electrons	Coin
Unobserved
Field of Probabilities
All Outcomes Exist		
Observed State	Hydrogen Helium	
Measured
Definite Location
One Specific Outcome	● Proton, P (positive charge, nuclear particle)
● Neutron, N (neutral charge, nuclear particle)
○ Electron, E (negative charge, orbits nucleus)	

This brings us to one of the most astonishing discoveries in modern science: the observer effect—the idea that the very act of observing something can alter its behavior. Take light, for instance: When unmeasured, it moves like a wave, but the moment we observe it, it behaves like a particle. Reality, it seems, is not entirely separate from the consciousness perceiving it. I first encountered this idea in a high school physics class, and it flipped my understanding of the world. It wasn't just a scientific revelation—it was a spiritual one. I realized that the way we witness the world changes the world. Our attention isn't neutral; it's creative.

The Double-Slit Experiment

The double-slit experiment, first performed by Thomas Young in 1801, is one of the most famous experiments in physics. Young directed light through two narrow slits and observed the resulting pattern. Instead of seeing two bands of light, he saw an interference pattern that showed light was behaving as a wave. This discovery challenged the particle theory of light and paved the way for quantum mechanics.

If light were a particle, you would expect to see two slits of light on a viewing screen after the light passes through two narrow slits.

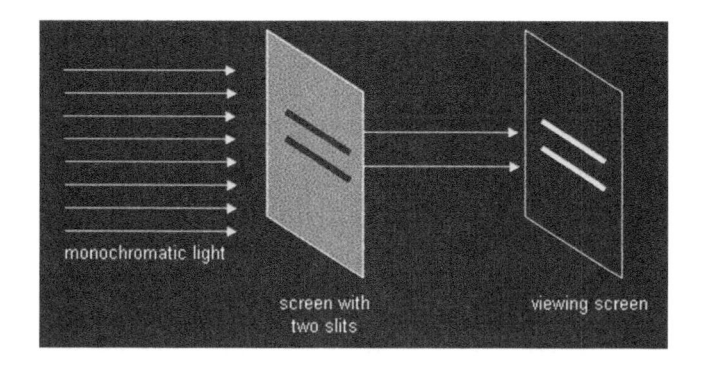

![Diagram showing monochromatic light passing through a screen with two slits, projecting two lines onto a viewing screen.]

monochromatic light — screen with two slits — viewing screen

However, if light were waves, we would see multiple lines on the viewing screen because the light would radiate from each slit in a wave pattern, and the overlapping set of waves would create an interference pattern where the light is canceled out in some areas and doubled in others. This interference pattern is no different in its mechanics than sets of ripples on the surface of water from two pebbles dropped at the same time.

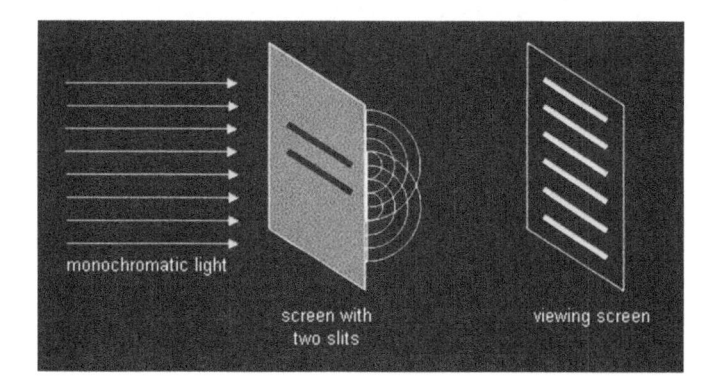

![Diagram showing monochromatic light passing through a screen with two slits, creating a wave interference pattern with multiple lines on the viewing screen.]

monochromatic light — screen with two slits — viewing screen

Later, the experiment was repeated with particles like electrons. In this setup, electrons behaved in the same way as light, producing an interference pattern that indicated they existed as waves. What's truly mind-boggling is that when an observer measures the particles to determine which slit the particle went through, the interference pattern disappears, and the particles behave as solid matter, following a predictable path. The act of observation collapses the wave of probabilities into a single, tangible reality simply by the act of observation. This finding led to the development of the wave-particle duality theory, which posits that particles can behave as both waves and particles depending on whether they are being observed. This reveals that the presence of an observer is intrinsic to the materialization of events in our universe, emphasizing the power of consciousness to shape the world around us.

Eckhart Tolle's insight into the nature of reality deepens our understanding of this connection between consciousness and the material world. He stated in his incredible book *A New Earth*, "You are not IN the universe, you ARE the universe, an intrinsic part of it. Ultimately you are not a person, but a focal point where the universe is becoming conscious of itself. What an amazing miracle." Tolle highlights the interconnectedness revealed by quantum theory, emphasizing that everything in the universe is linked through an invisible thread. This interconnectedness is not merely a theoretical idea but a living, dynamic reality that is shaped by the awareness we bring to it. Just as the quantum world reveals that particles are influenced by observation, our own awareness plays a critical role in creating and shaping the experiences we encounter.

We are a field of energy and information, constantly influencing our environment and being influenced by it. Our consciousness and the energy fields we create are fundamental to shaping the physical reality we experience. We are not passive observers of reality but active participants in its creation. Our thoughts, emotions, and intentions influence the energetic field around us, affecting both our internal and external worlds. In recognizing this, we can harness our ability to shape our reality, aligning our consciousness with the flow of energy to create meaningful change in our lives.

Unlocking Infinite Possibilities

When we apply the principles of quantum mechanics to our daily lives, we see that every decision, action, and thought is akin to opening Schrödinger's box. Each choice we make collapses a wave of potential into a single, tangible reality. This understanding opens up the possibility of living more consciously, recognizing that our attention, intention, and perception shape the world we experience.

By expanding our awareness of what is possible—shifting limiting beliefs, embracing new perspectives, and letting go of outdated attachments—we open ourselves to new timelines and possibilities. This is why personal growth and transformation are so powerful: they allow us to break free from old mental frameworks at the quantum level and create new realities that align more closely with our true potential.

Unity and Quantum Entanglement

The deeper I explored, the more it became clear that everything is connected in ways that defy ordinary logic. Quantum entanglement shattered even more assumptions I held about the nature of reality. In this phenomenon, two particles that become entangled remain mysteriously linked—so that a change in one instantaneously affects the other, no matter the distance between them. This isn't speculation; it has been repeatedly confirmed through experiment. Before such discoveries, it was widely believed that nothing in the universe could transmit information faster than the speed of light. If the universe were a computer, its maximum processing speed would be capped by that constant. But quantum entanglement revealed something far more astonishing: Particles separated by light-years can influence each other instantly, as if distance doesn't exist at all. It suggests that the universe is deeply unified—perhaps even conscious—and that information, or maybe consciousness itself, can transcend space entirely.

Entanglement scientifically demonstrates that everything has the potential to be intrinsically connected. What we think, feel, or do ripples through the fabric of reality, affecting not just our own lives, but also the collective experience of all. This interconnectedness is also mirrored in spiritual teachings, which emphasize that we are all part of a larger whole. Our thoughts and actions are not isolated—they are part of a vast, interconnected web that binds the universe together.

The Energy of Identity and Attachment

At the heart of the human experience is identity—how we see ourselves and how we attach meaning to our lives. Our identity shapes how we interact with the world and how we perceive our place within it. However, many of the beliefs tied to our identity are outdated or limiting, preventing us from expanding our potential. When we hold tightly to an identity formed by past experiences or societal expectations, we limit the possibilities available to us.

Quantum theory argues that reality is fluid, constantly shifting in response to our consciousness. Just as the double-slit experiment demonstrates the malleability of particles, we, too, can shift our personal realities by changing our focus, our attention, and our beliefs. Our identity is not a fixed state—it is a dynamic, evolving field that can expand to encompass new possibilities.

Aligning with the Flow of the Universe

Ultimately, what quantum physics taught me is this: Life flows most effortlessly when we stop trying to force it into rigid expectations and instead align ourselves with possibility. The universe is not a fixed machine; it's a living, breathing field of energy, constantly responding to the frequency of our consciousness. When we trust this field—when we tune into gratitude, creativity, openness, and love—we move into resonance with it. We stop fighting the current and start moving with it, and life begins to unfold with a surprising sense of ease and synchronicity.

I've seen it firsthand. When I approached life from a place of rigidity—demanding outcomes, clinging to labels, needing certainty—everything felt like a grind. Opportunities seemed scarce. The world looked heavy, like a closed door. But when I softened, when I allowed curiosity and trust to lead the way, doors I hadn't even seen before began swinging open. The universe seemed to rise up and meet me halfway, offering paths and connections I couldn't have scripted if I tried.

This shift isn't about pretending challenges don't exist or spiritually bypassing reality. It's about recognizing that life responds most beautifully when we become participants in its unfolding, not controllers of it. When we release our tight grip on how we think things should look, we create space for something even greater to emerge—something often better than we could have planned.

Quantum physics, spirituality, and direct life experience all whisper the same truth: You are not a passive observer moving through a static world. You are a co-creator, woven into the very fabric of existence. Your thoughts, intentions, and emotions don't just echo in your private mind; they ripple outward, touching the field around you, influencing the possibilities that appear.

Living in alignment means living from the inside out. It means remembering that you are connected to the source of creation itself—and that every moment, every breath, every decision is an opportunity to choose the frequency you want to embody. When you embody trust, gratitude, and authenticity, the external world shifts in response. Life becomes less about striving and more about attuning. It becomes less about chasing fulfillment "out there" and more about radiating it from within.

We are quantum beings, in a quantum universe. Every moment is not just happening to us—it's happening through us. Each thought, each act of love, each moment of clarity collapses possibilities into reality. The more consciously we live, the more beautiful the realities we help bring into form.

Core Messages

1. **The outer world is a mirror of your inner world.** Everything you encounter—people, events, challenges—is reflecting your consciousness back to you.

2. **Observation is creation.** What you focus on collapses possibility into form; your awareness shapes the version of reality you experience.

3. **You are not separate from the universe—you are entangled with it.** Just like quantum particles, your thoughts and emotions ripple through the field of reality, affecting both you and the collective.

4. **Identity is fluid, not fixed.** Letting go of outdated attachments to who you think you are creates space for new timelines and transformations to emerge.

5. **Living in alignment means resonating with the field of possibility, not controlling it.** Trust, gratitude, and presence allow life to unfold with grace and synchronicity.

Affirmations

1. "I am the observer and the creator of my reality."

2. "Everything I encounter is a reflection guiding me toward greater awareness."

3. "I release attachment to rigid identities and open to new possibilities."

4. "My consciousness is deeply connected to the fabric of the universe."

5. "I trust the unfolding of my life and align with its natural rhythm."

Practice: "The Mirror Room"

Objective: Discover how your outer world reflects your inner world.

Time: One hour (initial reflection), plus real-life tracking.

Steps:

1. Create a Mirror Map:

On a sheet of paper, draw 4 columns:

- *People who annoy me*
- *People who inspire me*
- *Situations I avoid*
- *Places where I thrive*

2. Write Down 2–3 Items per Column:

Then ask for each:

- *What part of myself does this reflect or challenge?*
- *What belief or behavior might be attracting this?*

3. In Practice:

Over the next week, notice real-world examples of how your energy is mirrored—especially in interactions.

Why it works: It makes the observer effect practical—helping you notice how your beliefs shape your world in real time.

CHAPTER 5

Reflections of Unity

What we project outward is often a mirror of our inner consciousness, but here's the profound part: What we experience is not only a reflection of ourselves—it is also the reality we collectively create. I began to realize that I wasn't just walking through life alone, but was, in fact, a co-creator of my reality, alongside everyone else around me. And this was a humbling truth to grasp and yet another step of discovery as I unwound the questions of who am I and what is this place.

As I reflected more on this, it became clear that this creative power isn't something we hold individually—it's something we share with others. Each person is a creator in their own right, and when we connect with others, our creative powers intermingle and our timelines intersect. At first, this concept was difficult for me to understand. It seemed like a lofty, abstract idea. But as I observed the way my own thoughts and actions influenced those around me (and vice versa), I began to feel this truth more deeply. We are all made of the same creative energy, flowing from the same universal source. We are not just separate entities, but interconnected expressions of one vast, cosmic consciousness.

In the beginning, I didn't fully grasp the depth of this. I would see how some people seemed so aware of their power to shape their lives, while others, including myself at times, seemed unaware of it. But the more I looked inward and observed the world around me, the more I began to understand: This shared energy, this collective consciousness, shapes everything. Our individual projections are not solitary—they mingle with others' projections, forming a collective experience of reality. It's a bit like sitting in a movie theater with others: we may all be watching the same film, but each of us experiences it through the lens of our own unique perspective.

The idea that reality is malleable, shaped by both individual and collective consciousness, was initially hard for me to accept. But as I began to observe how deeply the world we perceive is a reflection of these projections, the pieces started to come together. The roles we play—whether as parents, leaders, servants, or teachers—are deeply embedded in the collective psyche. These roles are like archetypes that echo through time, shaping how we behave, often without our conscious awareness.

Archetypes and Reality

Carl Jung's work on archetypes helped me make sense of this. I had heard of his ideas before, but I never truly understood the power they held. Archetypes, according to Jung, are universal patterns in the collective unconscious that influence not only individual behavior but societal narratives as well. For instance, the "shadow" archetype represents the repressed, hidden aspects of ourselves, while the "persona" is the social mask we present to the world. I began to recognize these patterns in my own life and in those around me. I saw how they shaped not only my actions but the stories we all play out in our daily lives.

Joseph Campbell, building on Jung's ideas, took this further in his exploration of the "hero's journey" in *The Hero with a Thousand Faces*. This concept resonated with me deeply because we see it in every form of literature, in movies, and throughout literary works across the ages. The hero's journey isn't just about the external challenges we face; it's about the inner transformation we undergo. The hero struggles with their own limitations, overcomes obstacles, and emerges changed. In the same way, we all embark on our personal journeys, confronting our inner challenges and limitations, ultimately gaining a deeper understanding of ourselves and the world around us. I started to see the patterns of my own life in the framework of the hero's journey, realizing that this journey was not just an external one, but an internal quest to understand and transcend the self.

As I explored this more, I realized that these roles and patterns aren't just abstract ideas—they're a deep, interconnected part of the reality we all create. The world we inhabit is like a grand, intricate tapestry, woven from both individual and collective consciousness. The archetypes we embody, whether we realize it or not, contribute to the ongoing creation of this shared reality. These patterns, though they may seem separate, are interconnected, like notes in a musical composition. I began to see how the world around me was harmonizing with my own consciousness, and how my actions, thoughts, and beliefs were not isolated—they were part of a much larger, symphonic design.

Indra's Net and Infinite Reflections

A powerful way to understand this interconnectedness is through the metaphor of Indra's net, an ancient symbol from Hindu and Buddhist traditions. I had read about this concept before, but it wasn't until I experienced a deeper shift in my perspective that it really clicked. Indra's net is said to stretch infinitely across the universe, with each intersection of the net containing a jewel. Each jewel represents an individual consciousness, yet these jewels are not isolated. They reflect one another, creating an infinite web of interconnectedness. Each reflection holds not only the essence of its neighbor but the reflection of the entire net. The more I meditated on this, the more I realized how perfectly it encapsulates the interconnectedness of all life.

At first, this idea felt abstract to me. How could something so vast and intricate be real? But as I began to see the world and my life in this light, I began to feel the truth of it in my bones. We are not isolated; we are jewels in the vast net of existence, each one reflecting every other. And just like those jewels, we hold within us the essence of the whole.

The Illusion of Separation

Eckhart Tolle's words began to make more sense to me as well: "You are not separate from the whole. You are one with the sun, the earth, the air. You don't have a life. You are life." For a long time, I struggled with the idea that separateness was just an illusion. It felt hard to accept, as it meant letting go of everything I had built my identity around. But when I began to see myself as part of the greater whole—just one thread in the vast, intricate web of existence—something shifted. I no longer felt as if I were an isolated being, struggling against the current. I began to understand that I was part of the flow of life, a co-creator in this grand, interconnected reality.

This realization transformed how I related to the world around me. The divisions I had once felt—those of fear, judgment, and competition—lost their grip. I began to see others not as separate beings, but as expressions of the same universal energy, just as I was. It became clear to me that life wasn't about competing for resources or validation. Instead, we were all collaborators in the ongoing creation of our shared reality. Every thought, every word, every action was a thread in the fabric of a greater whole, influencing the world around us in ways we may not always see.

But this awareness doesn't come easily. It requires courage to confront the patterns and beliefs that perpetuate the illusion of separateness. It's not always comfortable to let go of the ego's need for distinction. But as I began to shed these layers, I found something beautiful beneath them: the recognition that I am part of something much larger than myself. You and I are jewels in Indra's net, reflecting the light of each other and the light Source, connected to all that exists.

Core Messages

1. **You are not separate from others—you are an interconnected expression of the greater whole.** Just like a jewel in Indra's net, your consciousness reflects and is reflected by all others.

2. **Your personal reality is co-created through the shared field of collective consciousness.** We don't create reality alone; we participate in a dynamic, unified system of mutual influence and reflection.

3. **Archetypes and universal patterns shape not just your story—but the story of humanity.** The hero's journey, the shadow, the persona—these timeless energies operate within and through all of us.

4. **True connection begins when the illusion of separateness dissolves.** Fear, judgment, and competition lose power when we recognize others as different faces of the same source.

5. **Unity consciousness transforms your relationship with the world.** When you act with awareness of your interconnection, you contribute to a more compassionate, harmonious reality.

Affirmations

1. "I am a unique expression of the whole, connected to all that is."

2. "My consciousness co-creates reality in harmony with others."

3. "I release the illusion of separation and embrace the truth of unity."

4. "The patterns within me connect me to the timeless patterns of human experience."

5. "Each thought, word, and action I offer ripples through the web of existence."

Practice: "Archetype in Action"

Objective: Discover the universal patterns playing out in your life.

Time: 2–3 days of observation.

Steps:

1. Pick 2 Current Roles You Play:

Parent, artist, leader, rebel, healer, seeker, student, etc.

2. Name the Archetype:

For each role, ask:

- *"What story am I playing out?"*
- *"What are the strengths and shadows of this archetype?"*

3. Conscious Rewriting:

Choose one "shadow" trait (e.g., control, fear of rejection) and rewrite the script. Examples:

- *From "martyr" to "conscious giver"*
- *From "victim" to "creator"*

4. Act It Out:

Over 2 days, live from your empowered archetype. Watch how the world responds.

Why it works: Archetypes are collective patterns. Reclaiming them allows you to shape your role instead of being shaped by it.

CHAPTER 6

Relationship as a Portal

We live in a world filled with other people, and yet how often do we truly see them? Not just their face, their clothes, or their role in our life—but their essence, the light behind their eyes. Every person you encounter is a spark of Source, a unique facet of the divine mosaic, walking their own sacred path. And when we remember this, our entire relationship to the world begins to transform.

Along my spiritual journey, as I became more aware of my thought patterns, I noticed how often my mind defaulted to judgment. Not harshly—but habitually. *That driver is selfish. That person isn't very deep. So-and-so just doesn't get it.* I don't think I'm unique in this. It's a by-product of a brain designed to sort, label, and defend. But as I began exploring consciousness and the architecture of reality more deeply, a new realization emerged: Everyone is a soul first, and a personality second. And that changes everything.

We often look at the surface: behavior, attitude, demeanor. But those are just masks worn for survival or self-expression.

Underneath the masks, there is always something sacred. Even the people we struggle with the most are showing us a piece of ourselves we haven't yet integrated. If we let them, relationships can be doorways into deeper compassion, empathy, and understanding.

Seeing the Divine in Each Other

Imagine Source as an infinite sun, and each of us as rays—distinct in form, but born of the same light. That means no one is "more divine" than anyone else. Some may be more aware of their light. Some may act from a place of deeper alignment. But the core remains the same. The radiance is in all of us.

Think of walking through a forest. Each tree is different—some are tall and lean, others twisted, gnarled, broken. But all draw life from the same earth, the same water, the same sun. People are like that. Some are wounded, hardened, or closed off—not because they lack divinity, but because they've forgotten it or been taught to hide it. When we remember this, we stop expecting perfection and start looking for truth. We begin to see the divine spark beneath the mess, the sacred within the struggle.

The Humility of Not Knowing

Here's something humbling: We don't really know what anyone is going through. We catch only a narrow slice of someone's life. We don't see their childhood wounds, their quiet struggles, or the prayers whispered into the dark. When we judge someone based on a single moment or behavior, we miss the vast, invisible context that shaped them.

There have been people who rubbed me the wrong way—people I found cold, abrupt, or difficult. It was easy to write them off. But time and again, when I chose to lean in rather than pull away, something shifted. As conversations deepened, stories emerged: childhood trauma, recent loss, personal battles I hadn't imagined as part of their past. Suddenly, their behavior made sense. What once looked like arrogance or indifference revealed itself as grief, fear, or simply self-protection. I had judged a book not just by its cover, but by a single page—and missed the entire story beneath.

Practicing this kind of awareness changes how we show up. We soften. We stop needing to be right. We trade quick conclusions for quiet curiosity. And in doing so, we move closer to what empathy truly is—not agreement or approval, but a willingness to understand.

Honoring the Source Within Others

To see another as divine is not to ignore their flaws—it is to look through them. It's recognizing that every interaction is sacred, that we're never just talking to "a person," but to a soul wrapped in experience.

This doesn't mean tolerating harm or excusing bad behavior. Boundaries are sacred too. But it does mean holding the perspective that every person—friend or stranger, ally or enemy—is walking their own path back to remembering who they are.

When you hold that truth, your energy shifts. People feel safer around you. They may not know why, but they sense it—you're not judging them; you're holding space. And in that space, healing becomes possible.

Relationships as Mirrors

Every relationship is a reflection, showing you something about yourself—your fears, your patterns, your projections. That partner who triggers your anger? They may be revealing where you haven't made peace with your past. That friend who inspires you? They're reflecting back your own untapped brilliance.

The more consciously you engage with others, the more aware you become of these reflections. You begin asking: *What is this person showing me about me?* And in that awareness, relationships become not just social experiences, but sacred mirrors—portals for transformation.

Seeing the Spark of Source in Others

Here are a few ways to live this truth daily:

- Pause before judgment. When someone irritates you, take one breath. Ask yourself: What might they be carrying that I can't see?

- Speak to the soul. In tough conversations, silently remind yourself: "This is a soul in front of me." Let that shift your tone.

- Find the light. Even in the most difficult person, try to find one redeeming quality. It shifts your energy and often theirs.

- Mirror the truth. Compliment something real. "I admire your perseverance." "I see how much you care." Reflect people back to themselves.

- Practice Sacred Eye Contact. Take a moment in conversation to really see the person—not just look at them. Let your gaze carry the message: I recognize you.

A Unified Humanity

Imagine a world where we all did this. Where we saw each other not through the filters of fear or division, but through the lens of sacred recognition. Cooperation would rise. Conflict would soften. Society wouldn't be a hierarchy of worth, but a symphony of expression. We'd begin to solve collective problems not through competition, but through compassion.

When we remember that we are all cut from the same fabric, we stop tearing at the seams. We start weaving something new.

Every relationship is a sacred mirror, reflecting not just who we are, but who we are becoming. The challenges, the connections, the heartbreaks, and the joys—they are not distractions from the path; they are the path. Through the eyes of the Other, we glimpse the infinite facets of the Self. And when we meet each reflection with presence and awareness, relationships become something far more than connection—they become a doorway. A portal to unity. A direct route home to Source.

Core Messages

1. **Every person you meet is a spark of Source—divine, whole, and walking their own sacred path.** True relationship begins when we look beyond behavior and see the soul.

2. **Relationships are mirrors that reflect back parts of ourselves.** Our triggers and inspirations in others reveal what's unhealed or unrecognized within.

3. **Judgment narrows, but empathy expands.** Pausing to consider what someone might be carrying opens the door to compassion and connection.

4. **Honoring the divine in others transforms your energy—and theirs.** When we hold space instead of projecting blame, we create the conditions for healing and growth.

5. **Relationships are not distractions from the path—they are the path.** Each interaction is a portal for awakening, integration, and returning to unity.

Affirmations

1. "I see the divine in everyone I meet, including myself."

2. "Every relationship is a sacred mirror guiding me toward deeper self-awareness."

3. "I hold space for others with compassion, curiosity, and care."

4. "I honor the soul behind the mask and the story behind the behavior."

5. "Connection is my path, and love is my practice."

Practice: The 3-Day "Soul Lens" Experiment

Objective: Shift how you perceive others by actively training yourself to see the soul behind the personality.

Time Frame: 3 days (or more)

- **Choose 3 People:** One you're close to, one you feel neutral about (like a barista or coworker), and one you find challenging or judge frequently.

- **Set a Daily Intention:** Each morning, remind yourself: *"Today, I will look for the soul behind the story. I will remember that everyone I meet is a spark of Source."*

- **Observe Your Interactions:** Notice your initial judgments or assumptions. Then ask yourself: *"What might this person be carrying that I cannot see?"* or *"How would I respond if I saw only their soul?"*

- **Offer a Subtle Act of Recognition:** Reflect their essence in a quiet way—through a warm glance, a genuine compliment, or a moment of deep, nonjudgmental listening.

- **Reflect Each Evening:** Ask yourself: *What surprised me about seeing people this way? Did anything shift in how they responded to me? What did I notice about myself?*

Why it works: This practice gently retrains your attention. It helps you recognize that every person is more than their behavior—they are a soul on a journey, just like you. When you relate from this awareness, relationships become more spacious, compassionate, and alive.

Part III

SOURCE – The Infinite Now

"You are the universe expressing
itself as a human for a little while."
—Eckhart Tolle

CHAPTER 7

Merging with the Infinite

We've journeyed through Self and Other. We've explored how our beliefs, perceptions, and subconscious patterns shape reality. We've looked at identity, time, and multidimensional consciousness. And we've examined how relationships and external experiences serve as mirrors—inviting us back to deeper layers of awareness and authenticity.

Now, we arrive at the final section of the SOS model: Source.

Where "Self" helped us reclaim our personal power and agency, and "Other" revealed our interconnectedness and the reflective nature of life, Source invites us to remember the origin and unity behind it all. This is the dimension of consciousness that is not defined by personal identity or external reflection—it is what *is*, beneath all names and forms. It is the infinite field from which all things arise, and to which all things return. The Source within and beyond.

Chapters 7 through 9 are about anchoring into that awareness—not as an abstract concept, but as a living presence. In chapter 7, we begin to recognize that the separation between Self, Other, and the Universe is an illusion—that behind the diversity of form is one unified field of being. In chapter 8, we'll explore what it means to live from this unity consciously—to align with the Source as a way of being. And in chapter 9, we'll close with a reminder of your cosmic nature, your creative power, and the invitation to live fully, with joy, purpose, and infinite possibility.

The Eternal Present Moment

We spend so much of our lives reaching. Reaching for goals, for answers, for healing, for meaning. But what if the truth you're seeking has been here the entire time—waiting in the quiet space underneath all that reaching?

Source doesn't require us to go anywhere. It asks us to arrive. Right here. Now.

The present moment is not just a place of temporary awareness. It is the portal to the Infinite. When you slow down enough to *be*, without trying to fix, prove, or perform, something opens. You begin to sense that the moment itself is sacred. That underneath all your thoughts and emotions is a stillness that holds everything. That stillness *is* Source. It's not something outside of you. It's the spaciousness you return to when you stop identifying with the surface of your life.

So much of modern life pulls us into future-based striving or past-based regret. But Source is always now. It doesn't live in memory or imagination—it lives in direct experience. And when you drop into that space, even for a few seconds, you begin to feel a truth that's impossible to fully describe but deeply familiar. Like a home you forgot you were missing.

Unity Beneath Diversity

If you look closely enough, you'll start to see that everything—your thoughts, relationships, nature, music, movement, stillness—is expressing the same intelligence in different forms. Just like every branch and leaf grows from the same tree, every being and moment arises from the same Source.

In separation, we see difference and comparison. In unity, we see patterns. We feel rhythm. We recognize that the world is not random—it's intelligent. Coherent. Alive.

Think of the way your breath moves in and out, the way your heart beats without your instruction, the way flowers open to the sun. These are not coincidences. These are reminders. Source expresses itself not just in grand cosmic moments, but in the most ordinary details of life. The whisper of wind through trees. The laughter between friends. The silence after a deep exhale. It's all sacred. All interconnected.

When we say "merging with the Infinite," we don't mean losing yourself or dissolving into some impersonal void. We mean waking up to the truth that *you were never separate to begin with*.

You've always been an expression of Source—temporarily believing you were something smaller.

The Presence That Holds It All

Most people think of "God" or "the Divine" as something external. A being in the sky. A power outside of themselves. But Source is not a separate force you must reach. It is the awareness behind your awareness. It's the presence watching your thoughts, the stillness behind your emotions, the intelligence in your cells.

You've already touched it. In those moments where time felt like it disappeared. In the awe of a sunset. In the stillness of meditation. In the unconditional love you felt holding your child. That was it. That *is* it.

The more you attune to this presence, the more you realize: You are not broken. You don't need fixing. You are already whole. Already held. Already home.

The work now is not to achieve anything, but to *remember* what's already true. And to return to it, again and again, until it becomes the place you live from—not just visit in fleeting moments of peace.

Embodying Source

What does it truly mean to live from Source?

It doesn't mean leaving behind your human experience or pretending life is always perfect. It means living with the awareness that everything—the mess, the magic, the mystery—is held within one field of intelligence. It means meeting each moment with the remembrance that you are not separate from what's unfolding. Others are not "out there"—they are extensions of Source. Challenges are not punishments—they are portals. And life is not a problem to solve—it's a frequency to attune to.

When you merge with the Infinite, you don't dissolve—you expand. You speak with greater clarity. You move with deeper ease. You respond with love instead of lack. You make choices not just from thought, but from alignment. You stop needing life to be certain, because you're anchored in something far more powerful than certainty. You're rooted in truth.

Source is not an idea to understand—it's a presence to remember.

It's the spaciousness behind your breath, the rhythm in your heartbeat, the spark in your joy. It is the intelligence that spins galaxies and grows wildflowers—with no hierarchy between them. You are not simply connected to Source: it lives in you, as you.

Core Messages

1. **The Source is not outside of you—it is within you, as the awareness beneath all experience.** You access it through stillness, presence, and the willingness to simply *be*.

2. **The present moment is the gateway to Source.** When you arrive fully here and now, you step into the timeless space where the Infinite lives.

3. **Everything in existence arises from the same unified field of consciousness.** Beneath the surface of difference is a deep and sacred wholeness.

4. **Merging with the Infinite means remembering you were never separate to begin with.** You are an expression of the whole—not apart from it, but of it.

5. **To live from Source is to embody peace, trust, and deep alignment.** It is not about escaping life, but about moving through it with presence and purpose.

Affirmations

1. "I am a living expression of Source, whole and infinite."

2. "I access peace and wisdom through the present moment."

3. "Separation is an illusion—I am connected to all that is."

4. "The stillness within me is sacred and always available."

5. "I trust the unfolding of life, anchored in the awareness of the Infinite."

Practice: Presence as Portal

Objective: Deepen your connection to Source through daily moments of stillness and presence.

Time: 5 minutes (or more) daily

Steps:

1. Choose a Moment of Stillness:

- Sit, lie down, or go for a slow walk. Let go of distractions and turn inward.

2. Focus on One Anchor:

- Your breath. The sounds around you. The feeling of your heartbeat. The space behind your thoughts.

3. Repeat Silently:

- "I am here. I am now. I am."
- Let the words fall away as presence deepens.

4. Notice Without Judging:

- Thoughts may come. That's OK. Gently return to your anchor. You are not trying to stop the mind—you are remembering the awareness beneath it.

Close with Gratitude:

- Before moving on, place a hand over your heart and silently say: "Thank you. I remember."

Why it works: This practice trains you to recognize Source not as an idea, but as a felt presence. The more you return to stillness, the more you remember the wholeness that was never lost.

CHAPTER 8

The Unified Source

There are some truths so elegant, so quietly profound, that they seem to exist beyond language, waiting patiently for us to notice them. One of those truths has echoed across centuries and cultures, whispered through temples and texts, and still reverberates in the hearts of those who dare to look inward. The phrase is simple: "As above, so below."

A Living Blueprint

The first time I came across the phrase "As above, so below," I was tucked into the dusty, esoteric section of a used bookstore, flipping through material about ancient Hermetic texts. At the time, it struck me as beautiful but cryptic—an elegant line from some long-lost mystic teaching. It lingered with me, but from a distance, like something sacred etched on a temple wall I wasn't yet meant to touch.

Much later, while exploring the structure of the atom, that phrase came alive in a way I hadn't expected. I was thinking about how electrons orbit the nucleus—held in place by invisible fields, moving in rhythmic patterns, never quite touching. Then my mind zoomed out: from atoms to solar systems to galaxies. The same structural intelligence was at play. The smallest mirrored the largest. They weren't just similar—they were built by the same underlying rhythm.

It was like catching a glimpse of reality's blueprint.

From that point forward, I couldn't unsee it. Branching rivers resembled the veins of leaves. Lightning looked like roots split across the sky. Cloud formations echoed tree canopies. Mountain ranges mirrored wave patterns. Even satellite views of cities lit at night looked like star clusters. The design was everywhere—scaling itself across form, not by accident, but by intention.

It was Source, repeating itself in infinite expressions. A signature etched into everything. Not distant. Not abstract. But alive. Present. Patterned into the very nature of being.

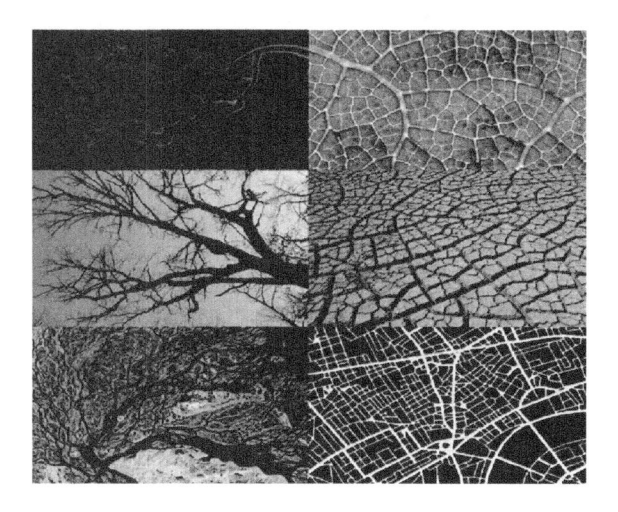

The Pattern of Expression and Return

This is the essence of the ancient Hermetic principle: "As above, so below." It's not just a phrase—it's a map of reality. It teaches us that the macrocosm and the microcosm are not separate domains. The laws that shape the galaxies are the same laws that shape our lives. What exists on one level of reality reflects and influences all the others.

This principle stretches far beyond Hermeticism. In the Vedic traditions of India, the relationship between Atman (the soul) and Brahman (the ultimate reality) shows us that the divine is not external—it is already within us, waiting to be realized. Kabbalistic teachings speak of divine emanations—sefirot—that shape both the spiritual realms and our daily experiences. These aren't just metaphors. They are living systems of knowledge, pointing again and again to the same essential truth: We are not separate from the structure of the cosmos. We are expressions of it.

Alchemy, too, taught this—transforming lead into gold was never just about metals. It was about the evolution of the self, the refinement of spirit. Astrology follows the same thread, mapping the movement of celestial bodies not to predict, but to reflect the rhythms of life. These systems, often misunderstood or discarded by modern thought, weren't relics—they were early attempts to articulate what science is only now confirming: that everything is deeply, intrinsically interconnected.

And this brings us back to Source—the infinite, intelligent field behind all things.

Over time, I've come to see that Source isn't just vast and powerful—it's also deeply curious. It's not detached or static. It explores. It expresses. It plays. It wants to know itself through every possible form.

This makes sense when you consider our own nature. Children, before they are shaped by culture or fear, are pure expressions of that curiosity. They imagine, they play, they create for no other reason than the joy of it. That's not immaturity. That's truth. That's our original state before identity, before pressure, before contraction.

It's no coincidence that we find joy in surprise. The unexpected twist, the joke we didn't see coming, the spontaneous insight that lands out of nowhere—these aren't human quirks. They're reflections of the cosmic impulse to explore the unknown.

Source expresses itself through everything—from the birth of stars to the sound of laughter. It creates lifetimes, not just to witness them, but to experience them through each of us. That means that your life, your thoughts, your sensations, your heartbreaks and victories—they are not random. They are expressions of the Infinite trying on the costume of you, just for the joy of experiencing and evolving in the process.

One of the ways I like to visualize this journey is through the shape of a torus—an elegant, spiraling loop of energy that moves outward from a center point, arcs through space, and folds back into itself. At the center lies Source—the origin, the unified field, the infinite intelligence. From that center flows creative energy: the pure expression of Source.

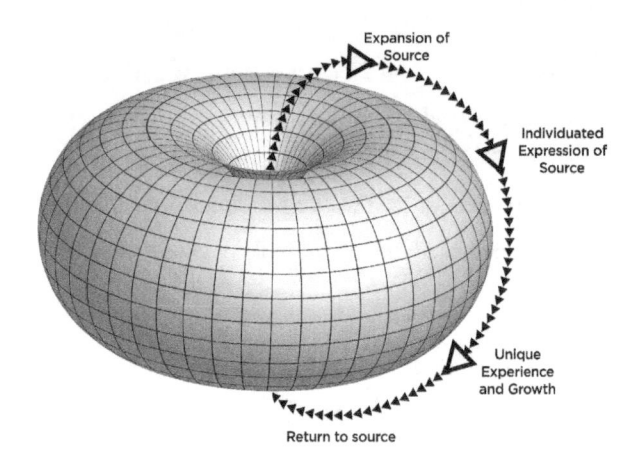

Expansion of Source

Individuated Expression of Source

Unique Experience and Growth

Return to source

As that flow moves outward, it differentiates. It takes on form, becomes individuated. This is where we find ourselves—distinct, defined, playing out a specific angle of consciousness. Here, we gain experience. We stretch, we grow, we explore. And eventually, that journey curves inward again. The arc becomes a return—not to where we were, but to what we've become. The return isn't a regression. It's a reunion, enriched by all we've lived and learned.

We don't go back to Source empty-handed. We return carrying the wisdom of contrast, the beauty of choice, the sacredness of becoming.

The Great Awakening

Something extraordinary is happening right now. Individually and collectively, humanity is beginning to awaken to the truth that we are all far greater and more connected than we could ever imagine. We are no longer content with the story of isolation. We are beginning to feel our connection—to each other, to the earth, to the cosmos itself.

Carl Sagan once said, "The cosmos is within us. We are made of star-stuff. We are a way for the universe to know itself." The more I've sat with that, the more I've realized—it's not just poetic. It's literal. When you ask questions, when you feel wonder, when you heal, when you love—you are helping the universe understand itself through the lens of your life. That is not small. That is sacred.

In many ways, this awakening mirrors the digital revolution of the 1990s—a time when everything shifted. We moved from fax machines to email, from pagers and payphones to cell phones, from card catalogs and quiet libraries to the infinite reach of the Internet in our laps. What seemed like a leap forward in technology was also a reflection of something deeper: the growing awareness of our inherent interconnectedness. We thought we were just building systems, but we were unknowingly modeling something timeless—the energetic web that has always linked us beyond time, space, and physical form.

This next revolution isn't about devices or data—it's about consciousness. It's happening not in our machines, but in our awareness. We're beginning to sense a field of intelligence that transcends what we can measure, a subtle current connecting every living thing. As we attune to it, we raise our frequency. And as our frequency rises, life begins to move differently—more clearly, more synchronously, more soulfully.

This shift calls us out of old paradigms. It invites us to stop striving and start aligning. To stop trying to dominate and begin co-creating. It asks us to step out of survival mode and into resonance. Because when we resonate with truth, with love, with unity—we remember. We remember who we are, and why we're here.

This is not a philosophy. It's a frequency. And you can feel it. In the ease that arrives when you speak your truth. In the warmth of presence. In the quiet knowing that arises when you stop performing and start listening.

Source delights in this remembering. Not just in your joy, but in your becoming. Not in your perfection, but in your presence. That's where the sacred lives—not in the distance between stars, but in the space between your breaths.

You are not just in the universe. The universe is in you. And when you live from that knowing, you don't just awaken—you become the awakening itself.

Core Messages

1. **"As above, so below" is not just wisdom—it's a blueprint of reality.** The micro and macro reflect each other because they are built from the same intelligent Source.

2. **Everything in nature mirrors divine structure.** From atoms to galaxies, rivers to neurons—every layer of reality carries the same sacred pattern.

3. **Source expresses through you as a way to know itself.** Your life is not random—it is a living, evolving expression of universal curiosity and creativity.

4. **You are on a journey from unity, into form, and back again—with wisdom gained along the way.** This is not a cycle of forgetting, but of deepening remembrance and conscious return.

5. **The awakening of humanity is a shift in frequency, not philosophy.** This global transformation calls us to co-create from love, resonance, and truth.

Affirmations

1. "I am an expression of Source, created from the same intelligence as the stars."

2. "As above, so below—my inner world reflects the cosmos."

3. "I carry the sacred pattern of the universe within me."

4. "My life is a bridge between form and spirit, between curiosity and creation."

5. "I align with the frequency of unity, truth, and joy."

Practice: Living the Blueprint

Objective: Notice and embody the "as above, so below" pattern through your daily life—linking personal experience to cosmic design.

Time Frame: 1 day of awareness (can be repeated anytime)

- **Morning Reflection (5–10 minutes):**
    - Begin the day by sitting quietly and asking: *"What might Source be learning through me today?"* or *"How can I embody the larger pattern in the small choices I make?"* Let the question echo—don't force an answer. Just listen.

- **Throughout the Day:**
    - As you go about normal activities, notice patterns that mirror cosmic principles:
        - Breathing in and out (flow and return)
        - Giving and receiving energy in conversations
        - Cycles in your mood, thoughts, or creativity

- Symmetry or fractals in your environment (food, architecture, nature)
  - Let each pattern remind you: *This is not separate from the cosmos. I am part of the design.*

- **Evening Journaling (10 minutes):**
  - Reflect on your day. Ask:
    - *Where did I feel most connected to something larger than myself?*
    - *What did I give today? What did I receive?*
    - *Where did I resist the flow? Where did I align with it?*
    - *What wisdom did Source gain through me today?*
    - Let your answers emerge without judgment.

Why it works: This practice makes the abstract tangible. It helps you move from *thinking about* universal truths to *living* them. As above, so below—your ordinary life is already a reflection of the extraordinary. Awareness turns it sacred.

CHAPTER 9

Living the Sacred Pattern

In the vast, ever-unfolding tapestry of existence, a profound truth emerges: While Source is infinite and indivisible, it is also constantly expressing, endlessly evolving through its radiant extensions—those sacred sparks of itself scattered across time, space, and form. We are each one of those sparks, and though we appear separate, each of us carries the full imprint of the whole.

This paradox—that Source is both eternally complete and yet always becoming—is not one to be solved, but to be lived. Each experience, each moment of awakening, every sorrow weathered and every joy embraced—all of it becomes a note in the great song of becoming. In this sense, your life is not merely a personal path, but an offering to the evolution of the cosmos itself. Your insights are Source learning more about itself. Your healing, Source remembering wholeness. The sacred paradox is this: while Source is already complete, it still evolves—through your becoming.

The Fractal Nature of Consciousness

A fractal is a pattern that repeats itself at every scale—zoom in or zoom out, and you'll find the same structure, the same rhythm.

You've probably seen them without realizing it: in the frost on your window, in the curl of a seashell, in the way tree branches split and spread. They show up in your morning coffee's swirls, in satellite images of rivers and coastlines, even in the crackling flash of lightning. Fractals feel familiar because they are familiar—they mirror the deep architecture of the universe itself, and of you.

Fractals offer us a lens through which to understand this divine paradox. In their intricate, self-repeating patterns lies a metaphor so rich that it reaches from the deepest recesses of mathematical thought to every corner of the physical world. The word *fractal*, derived from the Latin *frāctus*, meaning "broken" or "fractured," speaks not of disarray, but of unity made visible through diversity. The pattern of the whole expressed through the part, again and again, across scale.

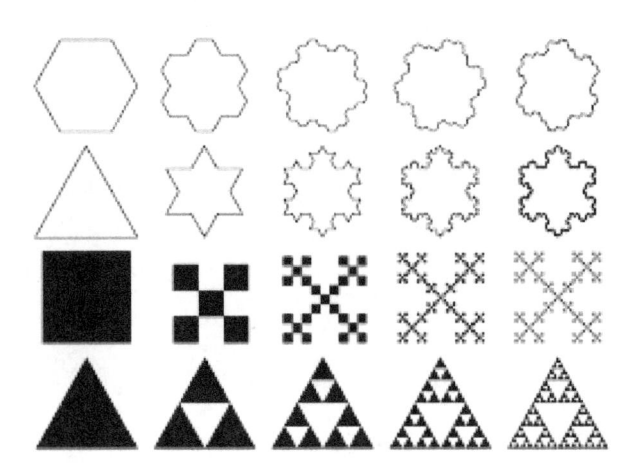

These aren't metaphors. They are signatures—repeating shapes that stretch from the smallest particle to the largest structure in the universe. They remind us that everything is connected, and that connection is not symbolic. It is structural. Fundamental.

Mathematician Benoit Mandelbrot popularized the concept in 1980 through what is now known as the Mandelbrot set—a mesmerizing visual representation of how simple formulas can birth infinite complexity. But long before equations captured their forms, fractals had been quietly organizing the architecture of nature. This intelligence doesn't just shape nature—it weaves through everything. From biology to city grids, from weather to art, the same fractal essence emerges, revealing an invisible thread of unity running through all forms of existence.

Images of fractals in mathematics and nature show us what our intuition already knows: that everything is connected, that the smallest mirrors the largest, and that we are made of the very same patterning that governs galaxies and atoms alike. Thus, "As above, so below" is truly an expression of the fractal nature of consciousness and our physical universe.

In this way, consciousness too is fractal. Your thoughts, your inner experiences, your growth and transformations—they are not isolated events but expressions of a cosmic pattern repeating through your life. When you shift your perception, when you rise above a limitation, when you heal even the smallest hurt, that shift echoes across the greater whole. You are not just living—you are imprinting your evolution into the geometry of existence.

You've felt it, even if you couldn't explain it: the way a room shifts when someone enters in deep peace—or deep grief. The way collective moments of sorrow or joy seem to ripple through the air, changing the texture of everything. These aren't abstractions. They are evidence. Consciousness connects us—subtly, powerfully, and without words.

Just as fractals reveal complexity emerging from simplicity, so too does your personal growth reflect the larger evolution of the cosmos. Nothing you do is insignificant. Every act of presence, every step toward awareness, ripples into the collective and beyond.

Personal Growth as Cosmic Evolution

From this perspective, the path of personal transformation reveals itself not as a luxury or private endeavor, but as a sacred responsibility. Your evolution is not separate from the world's evolution. Every moment you choose awareness over reactivity, compassion over control, or truth over comfort, you bring coherence into the field. You return harmony to a pattern momentarily disrupted.

Imagine a symphony in a grand music hall. Each musician plays their part, not to be heard above the others, but to contribute to something larger, something emergent. You are both the note and the music. Both the voice and the vibration. And the symphony grows richer with every return to authenticity.

Every time you move from fear to love, from reaction to awareness, from separation to presence—you shift the frequency of the whole. What may have looked like an ordinary life becomes a living prayer.

Jane Goodall once said, "What you do makes a difference, and you have to decide what kind of difference you want to make." The difference you make may never be charted on graphs or carved into stone, but the frequency of your life—the quality of your attention, the sincerity of your love, the courage of your integrity—leaves an imprint that is felt in ways you may never fully comprehend.

And so, the journey inward becomes inseparable from the journey outward. As you come to know yourself, you come to know the universe. As you awaken to your nature, you become a catalyst for the awakening of others. As you return to your center, you anchor more light into the collective field.

Demonstrating Your Authenticity

At the heart of this journey is the remembering of who you truly are. Beneath the roles you've performed, the strategies you've learned, and the expectations you've carried, there is something constant—untouched, whole, and deeply true. That is your essence. That is your authenticity.

Authenticity has echoed through every part of this book, not as a theme, but as a throughline—because it is the connective tissue between Self, Other, and Source. To fully embody it, you must experience how it lives at each level of the SOS model.

It begins with the Self—your inner world, your awareness, your truth. Here, authenticity is your anchor. It's the moment you stop performing and start listening. The moment you reclaim your thoughts, your choices, your presence. Wholeness begins from within, and it is from that place that everything else aligns.

Then it moves into Other—your relationships, your environment, your experience of the world. As you start to live more fully from your authentic self, you begin to recognize that same authenticity in others. You notice the aliveness behind someone's eyes, the quiet truth in nature, the resonance in synchronicities. You begin to sense that authenticity isn't just a personal trait—it's a universal signature. It lives in everything.

And finally, you arrive at Source—the field that holds it all. Here, authenticity is not just expressed or recognized. It is revealed as the very nature of existence itself. The universe doesn't just allow authenticity—it requires it. It's baked into the design of reality, like gravity or light. The more you align with what is real within you, the more life rises to support it. The entire structure of reality responds to what is true.

This is why authenticity is not a luxury or personality trait. It is the path. It's how you harmonize with the deeper intelligence that animates all things. To live from this essence is to live in resonance with the Source from which you came. Not in defense, but in expression. Not in performance, but in presence.

This path isn't always easy. It asks you to let go of what's false, even when it feels familiar. It might require stillness, discomfort, or the unraveling of identities you've outgrown. But what you reclaim is priceless: your original frequency. You return to life not as an echo of expectation, but as an instrument of truth.

And when you do, life meets you differently. The right people appear. The path opens. Circumstances align. Not because you've forced anything—but because you've stopped resisting what you are.

This book is a perfect example of that. For years, I felt a quiet pull to turn my spiritual obsession into something tangible—something that could help others. But I was scared. Scared to reveal the "woo-woo" side of me. Outwardly, I was a fairly average guy. Internally, though, I was overflowing with thoughts about consciousness, energy, and the hidden architecture of reality.

I thought journaling might help. And it did. Most of the ideas in this book started as journal entries, scribbled in quiet moments over the years. Still, the thought of writing and publishing a book felt impossible. And even if I were to do such a thing, I was convinced it was guaranteed to result in wasted time and embarrassment. The longest piece I'd written was my master's thesis, and that took years to accomplish (at least society would give me the stamp of OK for doing that). The idea of wrangling these thoughts into coherent form—then figuring out how to actually publish them—felt overwhelming.

Thankfully, I was willing to sit in those feelings and examine them in the way that the first chapters of this book explain. I used these feelings to introspect on my fears, and then dug into where those fears were coming from. I actively worked to replace these limiting beliefs with beliefs that I am capable of accomplishing any goal that resonates with my core self. The content of this book is my passion, and sharing it with the hope that it may serve others is my spark of inner joy. So, I got over myself by going within and identifying and releasing beliefs and internal roadblocks that no longer serve me.

I took it one step at a time. I gathered my journal entries. I created a blog account and used it to start writing posts that were intended only for priming the pump and getting comfortable with expressing myself for others to see. I was so relieved when my first posts had zero views but I also knew that was just a sign that I still was not comfortable with my authenticity being seen. Onward I pressed, despite those fears.

I realized that with every step I took to open myself up, new tools presented themselves. I realized I did not have to make writing some big ceremony. It dawned on me that I could simply pop open the notes app on my phone and use voice-to-text at any given moment. That helped me realize that expressing myself did not have to be planned or scheduled; I gave myself permission to do it whenever it arose throughout my day.

I also realized I needed to give myself more permission and space to do what I love. I had been so immersed in showing up for others—at home and at work—that I'd unintentionally pushed my personal passions into the margins of my life, saving them for rare "off hours" that barely existed. To shift that pattern, I did something I had never done before: I took a day off work and two days away from my family to attend a spirituality conference in Colorado. It was something I had always wanted to do, but had too many excuses not to. The moment I booked the flights, I felt an immediate release—like my system recognized I had finally made a decision that honored who I am and what I care about.

When booking the trip, I was pondering whether I should rent a car or just Uber from the hotel to the conference. I sat in that question and got a hunch, an intuition that it would be likely I could simply meet a fellow conference-goer and we could share an Uber. That proved true, in an incredibly surprising and profound way.

That morning of the conference I was ready for my plan to see if the universe would align and I'd bump into the right person. When I went downstairs, the hotel dining area was empty except for a few families with sleepy kids. My plan, my hunch, was proving to be way off. As I finished my breakfast and the eating area cleared out, I was about to give in and book an Uber for myself. I was looking down at my phone scheduling the ride when someone stopped in front of my table. I looked up and saw a person I'd said hello to in the elevator the day before. I could tell she was looking for the right words to start the conversation, almost like a look of "I feel like I need to speak to this person but am not sure how to start the conversation." After a brief pause, she asked what brought me to town. I mentioned the conference. Her eyes lit up. She was attending too. Within a minute of conversing, she offered to share a ride. Mission accomplished, I thought. That's when things became profound and gave me 100 percent confidence in how the universe will enable and surprise you if you take actions to follow your passion and authenticity.

As we rode together, she shared that she'd been into the same topics as me since childhood. She told me that the moment she saw me, she felt like she knew me. That she was looking for me this morning—not knowing why, but trusting it would be revealed. I told her about my book and how I was struggling to produce content and the fears of how publishing would be difficult or impossible. She smiled and said, "I self-published bestsellers on Amazon. It's not as complicated as you think—I can show you how." That gave me chills. It's like the universe was literally handing me the keys to unlock the doors I was too afraid to open. She was more than happy to help me understand the publishing process. She held a Zoom training for me and a few others, breaking down the entire process. She became my accountability partner, checking in on me for months. Her name is Lolita Guarin, and I am forever grateful for her wisdom and support. When you take steps to follow your passion and live in your truth, the universe really does show up for you—sometimes in the most unexpected, beautiful ways.

But the story doesn't end there. My first drafts read like a textbook—structured and covering the core topics, but missing something essential: me. I had faced my fears around organizing the content, but I was still holding back the part that mattered most—my voice, my stories, my truth. Friends and early readers all said the same thing: "This needs more of you in it." And that terrified me. What would people think? Would it ruin my credibility? Would it change how I'm seen in my relationships—or even affect my career?

Then I remembered what I believe: The universe supports authenticity. When we align with who we truly are, life has a way of responding—clearing paths, opening doors, softening resistance. I began to see that being fully myself wasn't just about personal healing or creative expression; it was an invitation for others to do the same. The fears I had about how writing this book might disrupt my family or work life turned out to be illusions. In truth, the more I honored my joy and followed what felt aligned, the more ease and harmony unfolded around me. Giving myself permission to write from my center—to tell the truth of my experience—didn't just transform the book. It transformed me. And my hope is that it does the same for anyone who reads it.

That's what it means to demonstrate authenticity—not just with ideas, but with action. To step into who you are, fully and without restraint. To let your light shine—not for attention, but because it lights the path for others.

Crossing the Threshold

There comes a moment on every conscious journey where the call gets louder—and the fear gets real. It's one thing to know who you are on the inside. It's another to let that truth be visible, unfiltered, and unafraid. Especially when the version of you that's emerging doesn't quite fit the molds others have known or expected.

For many of us, the deeper we awaken, the more tension we feel between the truth within and the roles we've been playing. Not because we're doing something wrong—but because we're expanding. That discomfort? That vulnerability? That sense of standing at the edge of something both exhilarating and unknown? That's the threshold. And it's sacred.

You may feel the fear of being seen. The fear of judgment. The fear of outgrowing your surroundings or no longer being understood. These are echoes of old survival strategies—ones that kept you safe in earlier chapters of life, but can no longer hold the fullness of who you are becoming. That fear isn't a stop sign. It's a signal that you're right on time.

You are not here to stay hidden. You are not here to shrink yourself for comfort or approval. You are here to radiate—to embody the truth you've remembered and to live it in a world that desperately needs your resonance. Your authenticity isn't just personal—it's planetary. Every time you speak from your center, you ripple a frequency that gives others permission to do the same.

Let this be your reminder: You don't need to be fearless. You just need to trust—trust your alignment, trust your inner knowing, trust that even if things don't unfold the way you imagined, something even more aligned is making its way to you. This isn't about blind faith or forced optimism. It's a deeper intelligence, a quiet certainty that the path reveals itself when you dare to walk it. Your path is not ahead of you—it's inside you. And the more you trust it, the more life rearranges to meet you there.

Embracing the Infinite Possibilities

And so we arrive at the threshold of choice—not once, but again and again. Each moment offers the opportunity to return to your center, to align with your essence, to participate consciously in the unfolding of reality.

As Joe Dispenza stated in his profound book *Becoming Supernatural*, "The quantum field responds not to what we want; it responds to who we are being."

This is the key. Not who you say you are. Not who you wish you were. But who you are being. In your choices, in your presence, in the energy you carry. The universe is not a passive backdrop. It is a living mirror. A responsive field. An intelligent force that listens not to your words, but to your frequency.

And this is where your true power lies. Not in controlling outcomes, but in mastering your state. When you embody the frequency of love, clarity, creativity, or peace, you draw those patterns forth from the field. You become a node of resonance, a lighthouse in the fog, a stabilizing force in a chaotic system.

Every moment of alignment is a fractal echo of the original creation. A return to the sacred pattern. A reactivation of the Source within.

The Next Adventure

Where does this leave you? Here, now, standing in the truth of your significance. You are not an accident of chemistry or chance. You are a deliberate extension of the infinite, intentionally here in this body, at this time, with these gifts and these challenges, for a reason.

Your presence in this world matters. Your voice, your perspective, your being—all of it contributes to the evolution of consciousness. And the more you live from that truth, the more life rises to meet you. This is not about perfection. It is about participation. Show up. Be curious. Stay open. Let yourself be changed by love, by challenge, by mystery.

And above all, trust: you are the cosmos, learning how to become itself, again and again, through the sacred experience of being you.

Core Messages

1. **You are a fractal of Source—whole within the whole.** Your life is not separate from the universe's evolution, but a direct extension and expression of it.

2. **Personal growth is cosmic contribution.** Every act of healing, presence, and integrity ripples through the collective field, shaping reality.

3. **Authenticity is not optional—it is your sacred responsibility.** Living from your essence aligns you with the greater intelligence of the cosmos and amplifies its harmony.

4. **The universe responds to your being, not your effort.** It mirrors your frequency, not your words; your state of alignment is what reshapes the field.

5. **You are here on purpose.** Your life, your presence, and your perspective are vital threads in the tapestry of conscious evolution.

Affirmations

1. "I am a fractal of Source, whole within the whole."

2. "My personal transformation contributes to the awakening of all."

3. "The universe responds to who I am being, and I choose to embody truth."

4. "My authenticity is a sacred act of cosmic alignment."

5. "I am not separate from the cosmos—I am the cosmos remembering itself through me."

Practice: "Ripple Mapping"

Objective: Realize how your personal growth shapes the collective.

Time Frame: 30–45 minutes of guided reflection.

Step 1: Identify a Breakthrough

- Think of a moment in your life when you experienced meaningful growth. It could be healing a relationship, overcoming a limiting belief, choosing integrity over comfort, or stepping into your truth. Write it down in a sentence or two.

Step 2: Trace the Ripple

- Ask: How might this shift have impacted others—directly or indirectly? Consider people you've interacted with since:
    - Did you speak differently to your child or partner?
    - Did you start showing up more honestly at work?
    - Did your energy, decisions, or courage silently give others permission to do the same?

- o Map it out like a web. Draw arrows or write short notes tracing how your shift may have rippled outward through conversations, relationships, choices, or creative expressions.

Step 3: Expand the Frame

- Now imagine each person you impacted carrying that frequency into their own lives—into their parenting, their friendships, their communities. Let the ripple continue.
- Ask yourself: *What might the world feel like if more people made similar shifts?*
- *What would happen if each person healed what I healed? Chose what I chose?*

Step 4: Anchor the Insight

- Write a simple declaration to yourself:

    "My personal evolution is not private—it is a gift to the whole."

    "When I rise, the field rises with me."

    "Each shift I make toward love, truth, or awareness sends ripples I may never see—but they matter."

Why it works: This practice helps you *feel* the reality that personal growth is not a silo—it's a signal. When you evolve, you broadcast new possibilities into the field of humanity. And while the effects may be invisible, they are real. You don't need a stage to change the world—you only need to change your state.

EPILOGUE

You Are the Source

There comes a point on any meaningful path where you pause—not because the journey is over, but because something in you has changed. A shift has occurred. A new layer of awareness has settled in. You feel it not as a conclusion, but as a quiet integration. A deeper breath. A steadier heartbeat.

This book wasn't designed to give you answers to memorize. It was a mirror, a set of keys, a transmission to help you remember what you've always carried: the intelligence, the agency, and the sacredness at the core of your being. If it offered any structure at all, it was only to point you back to the structureless truth beneath it.

Together, we've walked through the spiral of remembrance—through Self, through Other, and into Source. These aren't steps on a ladder or compartments of consciousness. They are facets of one living field, constantly reflecting and informing each other. You don't move through them once—you return to them again and again, each time more attuned, more honest, more free.

The journey began with the Self—the inner architect of perception, identity, and choice. Here, you remembered that your inner world shapes your experience, that your beliefs act as blueprints for your reality, and that presence is the gateway to transformation. You learned that your freedom doesn't lie in controlling the world around you, but in reclaiming authorship of the one within you.

From there, your awareness extended outward into the realm of Other—not just other people, but everything that seems to live outside of your skin: relationships, nature, situations, systems. Through this lens, you came to see that the outer world isn't separate—it's reflective. It shows you what's ready to be seen, what's been waiting to be healed, and what gifts are still waiting to be lived.

And then, finally, you touched the dimension of Source—not as a theory or distant divinity, but as the quiet hum beneath everything. The spacious awareness behind your thoughts. The creative pulse within every breath. You remembered that Source isn't something you seek. It's something you are.

These dimensions are not a model to master. They are movements within consciousness, weaving through you in every moment. When you learn to sense them, to live from them, life stops feeling like a puzzle to solve and begins to feel like a rhythm you can move with. You realize that the Self is not separate from the Other. The

Other is not separate from the Source. It is all one field, one flow, one expression of the same underlying intelligence.

To live from this awareness doesn't mean escaping the world—it means meeting it more fully. You still grieve. You still get frustrated. But you stop confusing temporary disconnection with permanent truth. You remember more quickly. You return more gently. And with each return, you become a more grounded presence in the lives of others, and in the evolution of the whole.

This is the real work. Not becoming someone else, but coming home to what you've always been. Not chasing perfection, but deepening presence. Not rising above your humanity, but infusing it with the awareness of what holds it all together.

So let this be the breath before the next beginning. Let it be the stillness where all the pieces integrate. Let it be the moment you realize that there's nothing missing, nothing broken, and nothing outside of you that you must become. You are already part of the pattern. Already in the dance. Already a vital thread in the fabric of what's unfolding.

And from this place, everything changes—not just how you see yourself, but how you move through the world. Not because someone told you what's true, but because something deep inside you finally remembered.

This isn't an ending—it's a return. A return to what has always been true, quietly waiting beneath the noise. A return to the center of your being. A return to the Source within you.

Printed in France by Amazon
Brétigny-sur-Orge, FR